PAINLESS, BLAMELESS & PEACEFUL

Orthodox Christian Reflections on Death, Dying & Eternal Life

FR. STAVROS N. AKROTIRIANAKIS

ANCIENT FAITH PUBLISHING

CHESTERTON, INDIANA

Published by:
Ancient Faith Publishing
A Division of Ancient Faith Ministries
1050 Broadway, Suite 6
Chesterton, IN 46304

Cover design: Amber Schley Iragui

Front cover art: Ruines du Chateau de Frauenstein, Friedrich Wizani, detail; © Bibliotheque Marmottan, Paris / Bridgeman Images

ISBN: 978-1-955890-86-1

Library of Congress Control Number: 2025942481

In memory of the children that I have helped lay to rest:

Ekaterina
Paraskeva
Katy
Ioannis
Bradley
Eleni Maria
Andrea
Stephanie
Alexandra Marie
Helen
Chloe
Nicholas
Nicholas
Alena
Elena
Mia

I promised their parents on the day of each funeral
that I would always remember them—
that their names would not be forgotten.

For everything there is a season,
and a time for every matter under heaven:
a time to be born, and a time to die;
a time to plant, and a time to pluck up what is planted;
a time to kill, and a time to heal;
a time to break down, and a time to build up;
a time to weep, and a time to laugh;
a time to mourn, and a time to dance;
a time to cast away stones and a time to gather stones together;
a time to embrace, and a time to refrain from embracing.
Ecclesiastes 3:1–5

For a Christian end to our lives, peaceful without shame and suffering, and for a good defense before the awesome judgment seat of Christ, let us ask the Lord.

~ A petition that occurs in every Vespers, Orthros (Matins), and Divine Liturgy in the Orthodox Church

Contents

Tough End-of-Life Decisions

The Role of Family in Death

At the Moment of Death and Afterward

The Funeral Service

Contents

Preface

The heavens are telling the glory of God;
and the firmament proclaims his handiwork.

Psalm 19:1

W hat will heaven be like? If only we had the answer to this question, it would give us motivation to stay on track in our Christian life, knowing what the reward will be. It would give us something to keep in our minds, especially when battling illness. It would help us let go as life ebbs away from us. And it would give us a good sense of our destination, keeping us moving on the journey.

The Orthodox prayer offered at funerals and memorial services asks the Lord to give rest to our departed loved ones "in a place of light, a place of repose, a place of refreshment, where there is no pain, sorrow, or suffering."[1] This is perhaps the best description of heaven, and I believe that God provides moments in life that give us glimpses of eternity. In my life, some of these glimpses came in the moments when I saw someone pass away—when the trauma of medical treatment gave way to a sense of perfect peace. I felt the palpable sense of angels in the room.

---

1 *The Divine Liturgy of St. John Chrysostom*, 3rd ed. (Holy Cross Orthodox Press, 1985), 167.

I've seen heaven in someone's passing, in some of the stories that I share in this book. While a loved one's death has sometimes been a traumatic moment for a family, over time they too reflect that it was perfect and peaceful.

Many times we experience this sense of perfection and peace in nature. A sunrise, a sunset, the sound of the ocean allow us to purge all our earthly thoughts and to revel in the beauty of nature. This, too, can be a foretaste of heaven. Imagine that feeling lasting forever. That's the end goal—a place of light, a place of rest, a place of refreshment, a place of joy in the presence of God, where that state never ends. That is what God has promised.

For some of us here on earth, worship is a chore. During the Divine Liturgy we might struggle to stay focused and concentrate. I celebrate the Divine Liturgy often, and each time out is not always profound. In fact, out of all the liturgies I have celebrated, only *one* stands out, where I felt like I was celebrating it in heaven, in perfect peace and perfect focus. I will always remember that Divine Liturgy, and when I allow myself to reflect back on it, I experience a hunger for heaven and a desire to work for that eternal reward with more conviction.

Psalm 19:1 reads, "The heavens are telling the glory of God; / and the firmament proclaims his handiwork." Anything that declares the glory of God—a sunrise, a sunset, lying out under the stars, worship, music—is also a slice of heaven.

We don't appreciate this—certainly not as often as we should. We get distracted. We take the good things and sometimes even the godly things, and we distort them because of our own sinfulness, our own brokenness. Despite all this, God is still great, and as long as we live and breathe, we have the hope of redemption.

We each live on a continuum between our earthly birth and our earthly death. Some of us are young, some are old. Some of us are in the sunset of our lives and know it, while some are in the sunset of our lives and don't know it. Some of us are close to God at this moment, and some are far away. Wherever you are, there should always be a sense of hope. Because with God, all things are possible. If a thief on a cross next to Jesus was redeemed and promised Paradise in his dying breath, there is indeed hope for all of us. The Bible is filled with people who failed but did not quit. Some of our greatest saints have committed some of the most egregious sins.

Wherever you are today and in whatever state of mind you are in as you read this book, go make something of today. There is a saying in sports: We play how we practice. If a team doesn't practice well, it probably won't play well when game day comes. If life is a practice for heaven, and heaven will be a place of light, rest, and refreshment, then we need to practice these things in life. We need to find places of light, rest, and refreshment that are godly and learn to enjoy them. And we need to promote, encourage, and share things that are light, restful, refreshing, and God-honoring with the people around us. When a team practices well, players look forward to the game, confident that they have prepared. When as Christians we have practiced our Faith well, we should actually look forward to our last day, confident and hopeful because we have prepared.

Christianity offers so many simple answers on how to live a life that pleases God and prepares us to enter into His Kingdom. Just taking the words of Psalm 19:1 and adapting them to our lives will point us in a good direction. If our lives are "telling" the glory of God, and if what we do "proclaims His handiwork," we will be in a good place for our final sunset, to close our eyes in death and open them to everlasting life.

Many people enjoy watching sunsets. We find beauty in the end of the day, when the last light of the sun paints a splendid picture across the sky. Yet I've never heard anyone lament the end of the sunset as the sky becomes fully dark. People walk away with pictures and memories of beautiful images—we are content and at peace, even though the day is now over. This is how the sunset of life should be. Those who are at the end of life, and those who are watching them, should be able to take away images of beauty, to find peace and contentment.

There are, of course, instances when there is no sunset—a sudden death or the death of a young person. For some people the sunset lasts for a very long time, such as when a family member has dementia. However, in many cases we know the sunset is coming, and it comes in a gradual way that is neither too long nor very short. It is primarily these instances we will address in this book. If God intends the sunset of each life to be a path to eternal life, then we need to find meaning and beauty in our personal sunset and in the sunsets of the people who will depart this life—to find contentment and peace even in the moments of sadness that surround the passing of our loved ones, and eventually of ourselves. It is my hope that through this book, we will understand that the sunset of a life actually can be beautiful, meaningful, and powerful, and we can walk away with images of beauty and not just feelings of sadness.

The following prayer comes from the Divine Liturgy of St. Basil the Great. It refers specifically to the Holy Gifts (Holy Communion) that are about to be distributed. If we replace "receive a portion of Your Holy Gifts worthily" with "reflect Your glory in all that we do today," we have a prayer that focuses us not only on the Divine Liturgy, but on everything we do outside of it.

Enable us, even up to our last breath, to *reflect Your glory in all that we do today* (receive a portion of Your holy Gifts worthily), as a provision for eternal life and as an acceptable defense at the awesome judgment seat of Your Christ. So that we also, together with all the saints who throughout the ages have pleased You, may become partakers of Your eternal good things, which You, Lord, have prepared for all those who love You. Amen.[2]

A sunset will come for each of us. If we have spent our lives proclaiming His handiwork, our sunset can be the heavens declaring the glory of God, and the gates of Paradise will once again open so that we can enter.

With love in the risen Lord,
+Fr. Stavros

---

2   *The Divine Liturgy of St. Basil the Great* (Holy Cross Orthodox Press, 1988), 38.

Introduction: What's the Why?

But earnestly desire the higher gifts.
And I will show you a still more excellent way.
1 Corinthians 12:31

A well-known saying in America is, "There is nothing guaranteed in life except for death and taxes." No matter who we are, no matter what we do, we are all guaranteed that one day we will die. As Christians, we believe that death is an exit from this life and an entrance into eternal life, heaven. But do we really believe that?

Obviously, no one is overjoyed to see a loved one die. Such a loss *should* feel bittersweet—the bitter sadness of someone we love leaving us, tempered by the sweet thought that our loved one will be with the Lord. In my twenty-seven years as a priest, I have often experienced the bitter side of death. I've seen people who profess to be devout Christians fighting to keep a loved one going on life support even when they've been declared brain dead. I've watched families become divided over the prospect of saying good-bye and keeping the fight for life going. I'm still told, "Father, when you go visit *Yiayia*, make sure you don't tell her you came just for her, because then she might think she's going to die." When I hear this, I always chuckle to myself and think, "Should I tell Yiayia that I just happened to be on this side of town, stumbling around the hospital, and randomly found her?" I even watched my own father, a devout Christian in the latter stages of cancer, struggle with fear of death.

I've watched people go to their deaths "kicking and screaming," both the person dying and their family. And I've also had the privilege of helping and watching people have a peaceful, memorable, and even joyful end to their lives. I've seen families who have been able to find sweetness in the midst of bitter sorrow. I've actually seen what I think are miracles happen, even though these miracles involved death—miracles like a dying person reconciling with someone he hadn't spoken with in years, or a family letting go and encouraging their loved one to go to God, so that both she and they were at peace. I've been in the room when people have passed from this life and have felt the palpable presence of angels.

Jesus promises eternal life to those who believe in Him. Heaven is a place where there is no pain, sorrow, or suffering. And while we shouldn't hate life or hope for it to end quickly, we should, on a Christian level, embrace death because death is the passage to eternal life.

Unfortunately, some people die young, from illness or horrific tragedy. I've experienced these deaths as well. This book will give only cursory reflections on those circumstances; instead, we will be concerned primarily with someone who is older, and we have a sense that death is coming. Both my parents passed away at age 78. Many people would say that is not old, and by today's standards it isn't. But my parents weren't young either. They had lived a full life, saw grandchildren, enjoyed retirement, and had both gotten sick with cancer. They fought valiantly and just ran out of "cards to play." The family had a sense that death was coming, and we took the time to offer a meaningful good-bye to each parent.

In every Divine Liturgy and in many other services in the Orthodox Church, we pray for a good death—a "Christian end." And yet when death comes, we often make it anything but good. I'm hoping to share some experiences, both good and bad, that I've had with dying people and their families. I will talk specifically about how we can accept death, help our loved ones accept it, and—dare I say—find some hope, and even joy, in death. Through the death and Resurrection of Jesus Christ, the Lord offers us a chance to go to the Paradise of heaven forever. Yet we shudder at the thought.

In several deathbed situations I will recount in this book, fear gave way to peace, and we could feel the presence of the Holy Spirit in the room with us. This reality motivates me to write on a subject we all will experience several times with people we love—and we will ultimately experience ourselves. Someone once told me that the most important day of our lives is the day we die, because how we die sets our path for eternity. Just look at the thief on the cross who repented. His whole life had been deemed worthless, as he was condemned to death. And yet, in his dying breath Christ assured him that he would be with Him in heaven, that very day. This book is written to help us understand death and prepare ourselves and our loved ones so that when the day comes, we will be filled with hope—that we can know sweetness and not just bitter sorrow at the prospect of death.

A Note on the Numbering of the Psalms

The Orthodox Church primarily uses translations from the Greek version of the Old Testament, known as the Septuagint, rather than translations from the Hebrew editions. The Septuagint (also known as the LXX) is the version of the Old Testament used in many quotations found in the New Testament, and the numbering of the psalms in the Septuagint differs from that found in Psalters and Bibles translated from the Hebrew. For example, one of the most prevalent psalms in Orthodox worship is Psalm 50 (in the Greek numbering).

In Hebrew numbering—the numbering used in most translations of the Bible—it is Psalm 51. In the reflections in this book, I will be using the more common Hebrew numbering for psalm references.

Format of This Book

I do not write as a theologian or in an academic tone. Instead, this book consists of my reflections on life and death as a priest who has had the privilege to offer pastoral care to hundreds of people who have passed away. I will share some ideas on how this end-of-life journey can be a more meaningful, and even beautiful, experience for all those who are affected by it.

The prayer that concludes each reflection will take one of two forms. Many chapters will end with an eight-verse excerpt from Psalm 119, because the beginning of the Orthodox funeral service contains eighteen verses from this psalm.[3] Other reflections will include prayers or psalm verses directly connected to the content of the reflection.[4]

Is there such a thing as a good death? I believe there is. And this is what I hope to share with you through this book.

Blessed are those whose way is blameless,
    who walk in the law of the LORD!
Blessed are those who keep his testimonies,
    who seek him with their whole heart,
who also do no wrong,

---

3   Psalm 119 is the longest chapter and also the longest psalm in the Bible, with 176 verses. The Lamentations on Good Friday, when sung completely (most churches do an abridged version) contain 176 hymns, each preceded by one verse of Psalm 119.

4   For simplicity, when quoting the Psalms I will use the common numbering from Protestant Bibles rather than the Septuagint numbering from Orthodox and Roman Catholic Bibles.

but walk in his ways!
Thou hast commanded thy precepts
    to be kept diligently.
O that my ways may be steadfast
    in keeping thy statutes!
Then I shall not be put to shame,
    having my eyes fixed on all thy commandments.
I will praise thee with an upright heart,
    when I learn thy righteous ordinances.
I will observe thy statutes;
O forsake me not utterly!
(Psalm 119:1–8)

The Orthodox Christian
Understanding of Death

The Most Important Petition of the Divine Liturgy

> When the Son of man comes in his glory, and all the angels
> with him, then he will sit on his glorious throne. Before him
> will be gathered all the nations, and he will separate them
> one from another as a shepherd separates the sheep from the
> goats, and he will place the sheep at his right hand, but the
> goats at the left.
>
> —Matthew 25:31–33

The Divine Liturgy is the consummate prayer. It covers every
kind of need we can think of—for peace in the world, our parish, the clergy, our country, travelers, the sick and suffering, good
weather, forgiveness, repentance, and so many more things that we
pray, not only for ourselves but for everyone. The Divine Liturgy provides a lens through which we can view the world. I may not be sick
on a particular day, but there are plenty of people in the world who
are sick, and when we pray for them in the Liturgy, I am given the
opportunity to remember, pray for, and show empathy for those who
come to mind.

At the center of the Divine Liturgy is the offering of bread and
wine and a prayer for God to send down the Holy Spirit upon them

to become the Body and Blood of Christ. The faithful then receive the consecrated Gifts in the Sacrament of Holy Communion.

One of the dozens of petitions that we pray is, "And let us ask for a Christian end to our life, peaceful without shame and suffering, and for a good defense before the awesome judgment seat of Christ."[5] This petition essentially entreats the Lord for a "good death." On any given day, we know that someone is at the end of life—it may be someone we know, or someone we don't. And just as we pray in the Divine Liturgy through a global lens for things like peace in the world, we also pray for a good death for everyone in the world, especially the people who will die today.

A Good Death

What is a good death? One that is painless, blameless, and peaceful, and one that is ready for a good accounting at the awesome judgment seat of Christ. Jesus reveals that at the end of time, a great judgment awaits every person who has ever lived. And that judgment will determine who goes into everlasting life and who goes into everlasting punishment.

We may or may not hear some of the petitions in our divine services in a personal way. I am not a civil authority or a bishop, so those petitions are never for me; they are my prayers for others. But sometimes the prayers are personal—I know people who are sick and suffering. However, this petition for a Christian end to life is very personal because an end is going to happen to all of us. I would argue that this is the most important petition of the Divine Liturgy, because when life on this earth is over, the only thing that will matter is the manner of our passing. Will it be Christian, painless,

---

5   *The Divine Liturgy of St. John Chrysostom* (Holy Cross Orthodox Press, 2015), 43.

blameless, and peaceful? Will we have a good accounting at the awesome judgment seat of Christ? At some point, good health, good weather, and even peace in the world won't matter to us. When we are on our deathbed, the only thing that will matter is this prayer.

Each time I offer this petition in a service, I make the sign of the cross, and I hear it in a personal way. As I begin writing this book, I am 51 years old. I am 2,500 weeks away from turning 100. I don't think I'll live to see 100; both my parents passed at 78. If I follow their track, I have less than 1,500 weeks left to live. And who knows? There is always the possibility that I will die in a car accident today. Suffice it to say that sometime in the next 2,500 weeks I am going to die. And so, as I hear this petition, I pray to God about my own death—that it will be painless, blameless, peaceful, and especially Christian. I pray that I will have done enough to be accounted worthy of a favorable judgment before the throne of God.

We would never take a journey without a destination. We would not walk or drive aimlessly. Everyone who goes anywhere has an idea of where they are going. Everyone who embarks on a project has an idea about its completion. Of course, there are always changes and surprises along the way, but there is a goal and a destination. In every life, the final destination is to pass away. Until that happens, the goal of our life should be to get ready by being a good steward—using our time and our talent in a way that glorifies God and serves others.

Ignoring Death

The Church is very wise in keeping this goal of preparing for death in front of us at all times, not in a fatalistic way or in a way that should make us sad, but in a way that should keep us focused and motivated. It is surprising to me that many people do not think about their own death at all—even people who are elderly. Adult children don't think about losing parents, even though this is the natural order. I can't tell you how many times I've visited people who are terminally ill or even actively dying who not only are in denial that they are dying but are confused as to why we die.

I remember visiting someone many years ago—and this scene has played out several times in my ministry—who was dying. As I visited them in the hospital, they asked, "What happens next?" I said, "You are going to die, then go to the Lord for judgment, and He will then place you where you will be for eternity."

It was as if I was speaking a foreign language, as if the dying person had never heard of the concept of death. I pointed out this petition of the Divine Liturgy, since this was a person who had faithfully attended church, and I said, "Where you are right now is what you've actually been praying for your whole life."

Death is a terrible thing, in that it is the ultimate negative consequence of sin and the Fall. However, there is hope, as physical death is the milestone by which the gates of heaven can be opened for us. Thus, we shouldn't be surprised, or scared, when the moment of death is upon us. The Church, in its wisdom, has set our eternal destination in front of us at all times—not as something to be feared, but something for which we are to prepare and actually embrace.

When you hear the petition "For a Christian end to our lives" in the Divine Liturgy and other services, pray these words for anyone you know who is dying, and pray it also for yourself. And sing the response, "Grant this, O Lord," for them—and especially for yourself.

How can a young man keep his way pure?
By guarding it according to thy word.
With my whole heart I seek thee;
let me not wander from thy commandments!
I have laid up thy word in my heart,
that I might not sin against thee.

Blessed be thou, O LORD;
    teach me thy statutes!
With my lips I declare
    all the ordinances of thy mouth.
In the ways of thy testimonies I delight
    as much as in all riches.
I will meditate on thy precepts,
    and fix my eyes on thy ways.
I will delight in thy statutes;
    I will not forget thy word.
(Psalm 119:9–16)

Death Is the Hardest Thing to Understand

But they do not know the thoughts of the LORD,
they do not understand his plan,
that he has gathered them as sheaves to the threshing floor.

Micah 4:12

Lots of things in life are hard to understand. Calculus, taxes, home appliance repair, how to raise a child—these are a few examples. Thankfully we don't all have to be great at advanced math, we can call people to repair our homes and do our taxes, and as for raising a child—for those of us who have them—we have our triumphs and make our mistakes, but we learn.

Losses are part of life. Some are irritating. For instance, when it rains and we lose the day at the beach we were planning, or our favorite restaurant is out of the dish we were looking forward to eating, these losses annoy us in the short term. But they are quickly forgotten. There will be other nice days to go to the beach, and our favorite restaurant will have our favorite meal another day. We know that. And we get over these losses.

Other losses are harder, because it takes a lot more to recover from them. When we lose a job, we often experience financial consequences. When we need to move, it's hard to build a life again. When the stock market takes a dive, it often takes years to recover. And when a marriage collapses, there are long-term consequences that, we hope, lessen with time.

The Hard Reality of Death

The hardest loss, and the hardest reality to wrap our minds around, is death. It is so permanent and final. There is no do-over. We can hope to buy another house, get another job, see improvement in the stock market, even get remarried. But when someone dies, there will never be another person like them. Both my parents are deceased, and even though I look to some people as a "mother" or "father" figure, there is no one else I will call Mom or Dad.

We know that death is part of life. People get old and they die. We know that children bury their parents. And yet it is hard to understand how and when that happens.

I was speaking with someone whose husband passed away from cancer only six weeks after he was diagnosed. He was just 64. No one in her family—not his wife, not him, not their children—thought that the previous Christmas was going to be his last one, that their vacation last summer would be their last trip, or that even six weeks ago, when he was diagnosed, that the end would come so quickly. And now everyone was left shaking their heads wondering how and why. We know that people get sick and some illnesses end in death, but why him? Why now? Why like this? I have known people in my ministry who were very health-conscious yet died in their 50s. And I know people who abused their bodies and lived into their 80s.

The only permanent loss is death. With other losses, we hold on to the hope that they can be recovered. But with death, there is no such hope.

Faith and Time

The other thing that is hard to understand is the destination, heaven. Where is it? What is it like? What will our loved ones be doing there? If more of these answers were known, perhaps death would be easier to grasp. If there were some way that our loved ones could communicate with us regularly—maybe send us photos—the unknown would be easier to bear.

This is where faith comes in. There are so many unknowns about the end of life and what comes next that either we live in faith, or we live in fear. Or we live without thinking about death, which results in fear at the end.

It is so important that we take time to think about death, because it is the common destiny for all of us. It literally can happen at any time. It can happen in a great variety of ways.

When we know death is coming, even if we only have a few days or weeks to prepare, it is important that we do so, for our own souls and for our families. For both the person dying and the family who will be left behind, it is important to say our good-byes and also to take care of practical details like wills, possessions, and funeral plans.

When death happens, it is important to take time to grieve. I will never understand why people think they have to be stoic when someone passes away. The Bible tells us that even Jesus wept for Lazarus. He stood in front of the tomb of His friend, and He cried.

In the grieving process, it is important to take time. A big and permanent loss—especially a sudden one—takes time to process. For friends who die, that might only take a few days. For family and close friends, healing will take much longer. Some people start to heal at the funeral. But for many people, especially those who were close to the one who died, the process takes much longer. Counseling or grief support groups can provide great benefit, not only to try to understand, but on an even more basic level, to cope with loss.

Managing Loss

And then there are the losses which we can't understand, like the death of a young person, or a sudden accident or tragedy. For these situations, the operative word becomes *management*—not how to get over the loss, but how to manage grief and still be productive, still find joy. I know, unfortunately, many people who have buried a child, including several close friends. I will never tell them to move on. I will never try to find an explanation for something for which there isn't one. Instead, I encourage them to manage their grief—to find a special place to remember a child while still experiencing the fullness of life, including love, joy, and laughter. The same could be said for anyone who has suffered the loss of a loved one, regardless of the circumstances: Take time to grieve. Manage what cannot and need not be overcome. Then give yourself permission to laugh and feel joy.

We don't have to completely understand death or master the concept of why people die. We simply have to manage our grief. Some things we will never understand, and that's okay. Death—the how, when, and why—is hard to understand, and that's okay. Some losses we will never overcome, but we can manage them.

And that's okay.

> Deal bountifully with thy servant,
>   that I may live and observe thy word.
> Open my eyes, that I may behold
>   wondrous things out of thy law.
> I am a sojourner on earth;
>   hide not thy commandments from me!

My soul is consumed with longing
    for thy ordinances at all times.
Thou dost rebuke the insolent, accursed ones,
    who wander from thy commandments;
take away from me their scorn and contempt,
    for I have kept thy testimonies.
Even though princes sit plotting against me,
    thy servant will meditate on thy statutes.
Thy testimonies are my delight,
    they are my counselors.
(Psalm 119:17–24)

Why Do People Die?

And to Adam He said,
"Because you have listened to the voice of your wife, / and have
    eaten of the tree
of which I commanded you, / 'You shall not eat of it,'
cursed is the ground because of you; / in toil you shall eat of
    it all the days of your life; thorns and thistles it shall bring
    forth to you; / and you shall eat the plants of the field.
In the sweat of your face / you shall eat bread
till you return to the ground, / for out of it you were taken;
you are dust, / and to dust you shall return."
                                            —Genesis 3:17–19

W
hy do we die? Why did God even bother creating us if we are going to die? These are fair, philosophical questions. God did not create us to die. He created us out of love, to share in His love. When God created Adam and Eve, He placed them in Paradise, the Garden of Eden, and there they lived in perfect oneness with God. The Bible tells us that they were naked and unashamed as they stood in the presence of God (Gen. 2:25).

Consequences of the Fall

When God created Adam, He said, "Let us make man in our image, after our likeness" (Gen. 1:26). The part of us that is like God is our soul—the part of us that comes to know God and is intended to be with God. God gave Adam and Eve free reign over all of creation, with one caveat—that they were not to eat from the Tree of the Knowledge of Good and Evil. God did not put the tree there as some kind of cruel joke or as an intentional temptation. God created us to share in His love, but love is a choice.

Love cannot be imposed or demanded. God gave us free will to freely choose to love Him, and He placed this tree in the Garden in order to give humanity this freedom. Humanity could choose to follow this one rule and remain united with God, or humanity could choose to break the rule and sever their relationship with God. Adam and Eve chose to partake of the forbidden tree, based on a lie from the devil, and this resulted in the Fall of humanity. Humanity had chosen to separate from God; God did not choose to separate from us.

A Pandora's box opened once sin entered the world. The perfection of Paradise, the bliss in which Adam and Eve existed before the Fall, was no more. Where there had been perfection, now there wasn't. For instance, before the Fall there were no destructive weather-related issues. But with the Fall of humanity, the environment became fallen. Now there was too much rain, or not enough, the gentle breeze became gusty, the pleasant temperature became too hot or too cold. Disasters began to occur in nature.[6] Earthquakes, floods, volcanoes, hurricanes, landslides, and other catastrophes resulted from the now fallen creation. Whereas before the Fall the land had given forth plentifully and without effort, now there was drought and flood, and man had to till the ground with hard work.

---

6   I personally refuse to use the phrases "natural disasters" or "acts of God," as some insurance companies call them. I use the phrase "disasters of nature."

The floodgates for sin were opened. All sin can be traced to a common source: a failure to love, a failure either to love God or to love our neighbor. The choice to eat from the forbidden tree was a failure to love God. This opened the path for failure to love our neighbor as well. Now, all kinds of sins against God and neighbor entered the world, such as hatred, violence, deceit, anger, murder, lying, coveting, unwillingness to forgive, impatience, and war.

Humanity had once lived in perfect unity with God without threat of separation, and the final consequence of the Fall was the most significant: Humanity's relationship with God was severed. In Genesis 3:24, we read that God "drove out the man; and at the east of the garden of Eden, he placed the cherubim, and a flaming sword which turned every way, to guard the way to the tree of life." Man would be separated from Paradise. This is the most serious and permanent consequence of the Fall.

Death entered the world, and since then most people get old, sick, tired, and pained until they cease living. When "the LORD God formed man of dust from the ground," He "breathed into his nostrils the breath of life; and man became a living being" (Gen. 2:7). But after the Fall, at some point for each person, the breath ceased and the body decayed and returned to dust. Death is also an act of God's mercy, so that we don't live forever in sin and apart from Him.

Upon death, the soul then went to Hades, where it was separated from God, presumably for eternity, with no more breath, no more body, and the soul no longer with God. Before the Incarnation and Resurrection of Christ, the prospect of death cast a dark shadow over every life because of its eventual end in decay and in eternal separation of the soul from God in Hades.

But God did not leave humanity in this state of hopelessness. In the next reflection, we will discuss the purpose of life and what God intends for us in life and in death. Other reflections will address why death comes in the way that it does for some people. The purpose of this reflection has simply been to discuss why death exists and why it is the common destiny for everyone.

Knowledge is power. Death frightens us because we don't understand it. These reflections will hopefully bring some understanding so that we can feel empowered to deal with something that will happen to all of us—to our loved ones and eventually to ourselves.

> My soul cleaves to the dust;
>   revive me according to thy word!
> When I told of my ways, thou didst answer me;
>   teach me thy statutes!
> Make me understand the way of thy precepts,
>   and I will meditate on thy wondrous works.
> My souls melts away for sorrow;
>   strengthen me according to thy word!
> Put false ways far from me;
>   and graciously teach me thy law!
> I have chosen the way of faithfulness,
>   I set thy ordinances before me.
> I cleave to thy testimonies, O Lord;
>   let me not be put to shame!
> I will run in the way of thy commandments
>   when thou enlargest my understanding.
> (Psalm 119:25–32)

The Purpose of Life is to Prepare and Graduate

For God so loved the world that he gave his only Son,
that whoever believes in him should not perish but have eternal life.

John 3:16

G od did not want us to live in this state of permanent separation. His intent was not for life to be just a slow march to death and Hades. So, God got to work on a plan for the redemption and salvation of the world—a plan that would have its end in Paradise, where people would not be consigned to hell but would return once again to the state of being that Adam and Eve enjoyed before the Fall. How could this be possible?

The answer is found in John 3:16: "For God so loved the world that he gave his only Son, that whoever believes in him should not perish but have eternal life." God sent His only Son, the Word of God, who is coeternal and uncreated like the Father and the Spirit, who participated with God and the Holy Spirit in the creation of the world and was incarnated in the flesh in the Person of Jesus Christ. This is what the Nativity is all about. In John 1:14, we read "And the Word became flesh and dwelt among us, full of grace and truth; we have beheld His glory, glory as of the only Son from the Father." In taking on our nature, Christ suffered the consequences of the Fall while staying obedient to God the Father. He suffered from hunger, fatigue, grief, frustration, betrayal, denial, abandonment, and ultimately death on the Cross.

Jesus never sinned. Yet, He died. He who never sinned still paid the consequences for sin. In the Resurrection, He showed that there can be life after death, and this life would be with God, as He ascended into heaven and sat at the right hand of God, having now opened a path for us back to Paradise. This is why it was necessary for Christ to come to earth to die for our sins—to open up that path to Paradise for us to follow.

In the years between the Fall and the Incarnation, God prepared the people through the Law, to put a sense of order into the chaotic and fallen world. He also prepared them through prophets and holy people who were present in every generation, assuring the people that something greater was coming. These people also died and went to Hades, which is why the icon of the Resurrection depicts Jesus going to Hades to lift up all those who were bound there, such as Adam and Eve, Moses, John the Baptist, and others.

Jesus told us that He will come back to judge the living and the dead. We affirm this in the Creed each time we recite our statement of faith. Like the Old Testament, we also live in a time of expectation and waiting. Like the Old Testament, we have order, but the Law is not Ten Commandments. Instead, there are two: Love God and love our neighbor. And in every generation, saints and holy people model what it is to do both. These saints, just like every human being, are also going to endure a physical death.

Life, Death, and Preparation

So, what is the purpose of life? Perhaps this would be better answered by defining some terms. We use the word *life* to describe being alive, the period of time we are breathing and living on earth. *Death* is when that period of time ends.

Allow me to redefine these terms. Let's define *life* as being with God. This is the goal of each day—to live a godly life—to use our talents and opportunities, to create meaningful relationships, and to grow in our knowledge of God and our experience in serving Him. The ultimate goal of our existence is to be with God forever. Therefore, *life* spiritually begins at baptism as we become children of God and inheritors of His promises, and this life continues hopefully for eternity.

Death is absence from God. We die spiritually when we sin, when we estrange ourselves from God. The ultimate indignity is not to stop breathing—physical death—but to be cut off from God for eternity—spiritual death. If *life* ultimately means to be with God in heaven, then *death* is to be cut off from Him forever and to be in hell.

So, what do we call the time we are here on earth? I would call this time *preparation*. We each have a finite amount of time on earth before death occurs and we pass away. So we prepare, then we pass and go to judgment before God, where He deems us worthy either of life in the Kingdom of heaven or death and consignment to hell.

Another way to think of life is to compare it to college. The purpose of going to college is to learn and graduate, then move on to something greater. No one attends school with the intention of never leaving. When I went to college in 1990, the administration called students the "Class of 1994" on the day we arrived. That was to emphasize to us from the very beginning that our goal was to graduate, and they even had a date in mind when that would happen. Using this analogy, God knows our graduation date—the day we will pass from life. We do not know that date. Some of us may live twenty years, some fifty, some a hundred, just as some people go to college for two years or four years or ten. The course of life and manner of death will be different for each. But the purpose for each life is the same as the purpose for each student: to prepare and to graduate.

When graduation day comes for the college student, the emotions are bittersweet. There is some sadness as a season of life ends, a period that for most people has brought some good times and good memories that can be difficult to leave behind. However, the greater emotion is generally joy that a goal has been achieved and a larger world is about to open up.

Likewise, death brings bittersweet feelings to everyone, not only for those left behind but also for the person who is dying. There is a sadness that life is over and that a friend or family member is about to leave our company. But hopefully there is a joy that a greater world is about to open for this person, a return to God and the state of Paradise once enjoyed by humanity before the Fall.

Death as a Door to a Greater World

I heard a bishop say once at a funeral that death is actually God's greatest gift to us. Imagine, he said, that we were stuck in one stage of life forever. Imagine going to college for years and not being allowed to graduate. Imagine working for decades but never being allowed to retire. Imagine getting older and sicker with no end to it, ever. Life would be cruel. Allowing a person to die is actually a gift from God, because death allows us to escape the fallen world—in fact, it is the *only* way to escape. That doesn't mean we should hasten death; I will deal with that in a later reflection. It does mean that when death comes, we should not view it as the worst possible thing in the world. It is bad for those left behind, but for the faithful Christian, it opens the door to a greater world.

Another priest once gave a sermon entitled "Four Existential Questions" that asked, Where did I come from? What is my destiny?

What is my purpose? What is the difference between good and evil? Let's answer these.

+ We come from God, because we are created in His image and likeness.
+ Our destiny is to pass away from this life in the hope of eternal life.
+ Our purpose is to prepare for this, and we do this by loving God and serving our neighbor, using the talents with which God has blessed us.
+ As for the difference between good and evil, this is the challenge of life: to understand what is truly good and godly and to focus on that, and to understand what is truly evil and what takes us away from God and to repent of that.

Understanding where we are going, however, helps us figure out what to do today. Any given day is an opportunity to glorify God and to serve others. If we spend a lifetime doing that, we will be ready to pass away and meet the Lord for judgment to be worthy to enter into eternal life. And if *life* means being with God, then the doorway of death is a passage from life to life.

Each day in school moves a student closer to his or her graduation day. And each day puts us one day closer to our graduation from life. Rather than be sad or scared, let's focus on death as a graduation, a passing to a whole new and better, perfect world. And let's do our part to prepare each day by intentionally acting to show our love for God and our neighbor.

When a student is preparing for the final exam, if they've done the work all along, they may still have some anxiety, but they can be comforted in knowing that they prepared well. It's the same thing as our years of life go by. Rather than be nervous for the final exam—God's judgment—instead live intentionally for God today, by loving

Him and serving others. Then be comforted that you are preparing as well as you can.

> Teach me, O LORD, the way of thy statutes;
>   and I will keep it to the end.
> Give me understanding that I may keep thy law
>   and observe it with my whole heart.
> Lead me in the path of thy commandments,
>   for I delight in it.
> Incline my heart to thy testimonies,
>   and not to gain!
> Turn my eyes from looking at vanities;
>   and give me life in thy ways.
> Confirm to Thy servant thy promise,
>   which is for those who fear thee.
> Turn away the reproach which I dread;
>   for thy ordinances are good.
> Behold, I long for thy precepts;
>   in thy righteousness give me life.
> (Psalm 119:33–40)

A Different Course of Life for Each

For it will be as when a man going on a journey called his servants and entrusted to them his property; to one he gave five talents, to another two, to another one, to each according to his ability.

Matthew 25:14–15

In the last reflection, we compared life and its end to a student attending college, graduating, and going on to something bigger. Everyone who goes to college studies something different. Of course, many students have the same major, but if you consider majors, minors, and electives, no two students experience the exact same course of study. Factor in extracurricular activities, and we'll see that each journey through college is unique. What remains the same is that people finish and graduate.

Life works in the same fashion. Each of us is on a unique journey. I'm not the only Orthodox priest in the world. I might not be the only Orthodox priest who was ordained on May 15, 1998—perhaps another priest was ordained that day. I am definitely not the only Orthodox priest who grew up in the Los Angeles area. However, I am the only Orthodox priest who grew up in the Los Angeles area, was ordained on May 15, 1998, serves in Tampa, is married with one child, loves yard work, and writes every day. This story is unique to me.

Each of us has been given unique circumstances, abilities, and opportunities. With this reality in mind, one of the guiding Scripture passages for my life is Matthew 25:14–30, the Parable of the Talents. The parable begins with Jesus telling His disciples, "For it will be as when a man going on a journey called his servants and entrusted to them his property; to one he gave five talents, to another two, to another one, to each according to his ability." The *talent* is a large sum of money, what one would expect to earn in ten years. Each of the three servants was entrusted with differing amounts—no one was the same. If one talent is ten years' worth of earnings, even the servant who received the least still received something substantial. The most significant word here is the word *entrusted*—these talents were not given; they were loaned. The three servants were not owners, but stewards. A steward is a temporary caretaker.

Our Talents Are on Loan

This parable should speak to us all. Each of us has been given something substantial to offer the world. This includes our talents (abilities), our opportunities, the people we meet, even our very lives. Each of us will have different abilities, opportunities, people, and lifespan. No matter what I do with what I have been given—whether I double it, as did the servant with the five talents and the servant with the two talents, or whether I bury it in the ground, as did the servant with the one talent—at some point, the Master, the Lord, will return and ask me what I did with what He had entrusted me.

If you read on in this parable, you will notice that the master was equally happy with the man who started with five and made ten talents as he was with the one who multiplied two into four talents. He didn't ask the man who started with two why did he not end up with ten. He did, however, question and punish the man who had the one talent because he wasted what he had been given.

The goal of life is not to live to reach a certain age. It is to see everything we have that is good as a gift from God and to use what we have been given to glorify God and serve others. In very basic form, what we have been given is our life today. We're not entitled to anything, and we're certainly not entitled to live to be 80, 90, 100, or whatever society considers to be a good life. What we should be more concerned with is what *God* considers to be a good and godly life. We should be grateful for today. We should use our talents each day so that if the end comes when we are 40 or 70 or 100 years old, we can rest assured that we've done our best. And if we've done our best with what we've been given, what more can God ask from us?

When a clergyman passes away, the bishop offers a special prayer at his funeral. It speaks to death as being a great equalizer and the common destiny for everyone. It begins:

We thank You, O Lord our God, for Your life alone is immortal, and Your glory is incomprehensible, and Your mercy immeasurable, and Your love for mankind inexpressible, and Your reign without succession, and with You, Lord, there is no partiality towards persons; for You have required all men to pay the same debt when the full measure of their life has been completed.[7]

In a world that seems obsessed with equality, the Lord reminds us through this prayer and through the Parable of the Talents that it is not longevity that He cares about, but good stewardship of what we've been given. In the same vein, He does not measure our lives by

---

7   "Prayer by a Bishop for a Departed Priest," in *The Priest's Service Book*, trans. Fr. Evagoras Constantinides (self-published, 1989), 237.

how much we have but how much we do with what He has blessed us with. The prayer also reminds us that indeed we are stewards; we are temporary caretakers. Whatever we have is actually a loan—something God has entrusted to us temporarily.

God has invested in each of us, and He wants a good return on His investment. We won't all be blessed with 100 years of life. What matters most is making the most of the unique talents and circumstances that God provides for your life, and making the most of each gift, each day, even each moment.

Like the servants in the parable, each person's gifts are different. Some are doctors, some are teachers, some are parents, some are plumbers. What would the world be like if we had no sanitation workers to pick up the garbage? Disease would spread. What if there were no truck drivers? Food wouldn't get to the grocery store, supplies wouldn't get to doctors, medicines wouldn't get to pharmacies. We need all kinds of people doing all kinds of things to make the world function in a way that is healthy and viable. Rather than focus on what we do for a career, how much money we make, and even how long we live, we need to focus on what we do with what we've been given. What's important is not how many days we have, but what we do with those days.

> Let thy steadfast love come to me, O Lord,
> Thy salvation according to thy promise;
> then shall I have an answer for those who taunt me,
> for I trust in thy word.
> And take not the word of truth utterly out of my mouth,
> for my hope is in thy ordinances.
> I will keep thy law continually,
> forever and ever;
> and I shall walk at liberty,
> for I have sought thy precepts.

I will also speak of thy testimonies before kings,
    and shall not be put to shame;
for I find my delight in thy commandments,
    which I love.
I revere thy commandments, which I love,
    and I will meditate on thy statutes.
(Psalm 119:41–48)

The End Will Come in a Different Way for Each of Us

Each man's work will become manifest; for the Day will disclose it, because it will be revealed with fire, and the fire will test what sort of work each one has done. If the work which any man has built on the foundation survives, he will receive a reward. If any man's work is burned up, he will suffer loss, though he himself will be saved, but only as through fire.

1 Corinthians 3:13–15

Just as each of us will walk a different and unique path through life, with different talents, opportunities, and circumstances, life for each of us will also end in a unique way. Some of us will die young, and some will die old. Some will die suddenly, and some will endure a long period of illness. Some will die sooner because of their own choices or the mistakes of others.

Four Causes of Death

In my opinion, there are four causes of death:

1. **Our own mistakes.** If we make poor choices in terms of food, exercise, and behavior, bad consequences may follow. And

while there are some obvious bad choices, like smoking, drug use, or excessive drinking, plenty of people are working their way to "death by donut"—excessive eating. Bad choices like driving too fast or engaging in other risky activities can also bring about premature death. I wonder sometimes as I get older how long God intends for me to live, and I wonder if I am thwarting His intentions by bad diet. What if I die at a young age from poor diet and God says, "I intended for you to live to be 80, and you only made it to 60"?

2. **Mistakes of others.** If someone is driving too fast, hits my car, and I die, the fault can be placed at the hands of a bad driver. There are instances where God may perform a miracle and thwart the poor choice of someone who endangers us. But generally God leaves free will intact, and we often suffer the consequences of someone else misusing their free will intentionally or unintentionally. There will be further comment on this in an upcoming reflection.

3. **Disasters of nature.** We live in a broken world where we experience strong storms (hurricanes), plates of the earth that move (earthquakes/tsunamis), rain that falls too quickly in one area (flood), lightning strikes (fire), strong winds (tornadoes), and other disasters of nature. Just about every place on earth has experienced a disaster of nature.

4. **The human condition.** By this I mean that we all share a fallen human nature. Imagine for a moment, if you will, that four perfect people are sharing perfect conversation in a perfect room filled with perfect air. Then someone comes into the room and introduces a large amount of aerosol. The four people didn't do anything wrong. However, each is exposed to the aerosol and experiences a different consequence. One starts coughing, another starts sneezing, another gets watery eyes, and the fourth gets a headache. They are all exposed to the same thing,

they equally share the now imperfect air, but there is a different and unique consequence for each.

We equally share imperfect water and breathe imperfect air—though in some places of the world, the water and air are far worse than in others. We share imperfect gene pools that cause one person to have a lifelong learning disability, while another person who is in perfect health has early-onset dementia. Some people have high cholesterol no matter how healthy their diet is. Others suffer from different physical or psychological maladies. Some of the things we suffer from, especially mentally, are a product of our environment. And some are just innate. Sometimes a cause of death is explainable, and other times it is not.

In my family, both my parents passed away at age 78—they were eight years apart in age, and their deaths occurred eight years apart—both from cancer. Thus, there is a good chance I will get cancer and probably won't live to be 100. Armed with this knowledge and experience, I am more diligent about cancer screenings, although I am continuously battling weight issues. Maybe I will live a few more years than they did, unless something happens because of a personal bad decision, the bad decision of someone else, or a disaster of nature.

As I get older, I think about death a little bit more—not in a fatalistic way, but in a realistic way. I must admit that I am somewhat afraid of death—especially the dying process. How will that last chapter be written? I've seen people die in their sleep, and I think this is a blessing. If I could choose my way, I would choose that. I've seen people suffer from disease for many years, enduring a lot of pain along the way, and death came almost as a relief. I've seen other people who have dementia and who have forgotten who they are and who they love. This is another agonizing way to die. I've seen people who didn't shed tears when a loved one finally died, because they had already shed so many over a long period of time.

Hopefully I am living a life of faith and repentance that will put me in good standing at the awesome judgment seat of Christ when my time comes. Death will come in a different way for each of us, which is why it is important to remember the petition that is the genesis of this entire book: "And let us ask for a Christian end to our life, peaceful, without shame and suffering, and for a good defense before the awesome judgment seat of Christ."[8] Because the end for each person is so unique, we pray this petition as a general petition for everyone, in every circumstance.

Every successful life, and even every life that isn't very successful, has its challenges and rough roads. The road to the end of life will be more challenging for some than for others. This is why we have to keep our eyes on the prize of salvation, even when the road there is difficult and painful. We can only run our own race and encourage others to run theirs. And this is true whether we are in college, raising children, or walking the last mile.

> Be gracious to me, O God,
> for men trample upon me;
>   all day long foemen oppress me;
> my enemies trample upon me all day long,
>   for many fight against me proudly.
> When I am afraid,
>   I put my trust in thee.
> In God, whose word I praise,
>   in God I trust without a fear.
>   What can flesh do to me?
> All day long they seek to injure my cause;

---

8   *Divine Liturgy of St. John Chrysostom* (2015), 43.

all their thoughts are against me for evil.
They band themselves together, they lurk,
    they watch my steps.
As they have waited for my life,
    so recompense them for their crime;
    in wrath cast down the peoples, O God!
Thou hast kept count of my tossings;
    put thou my tears in thy bottle!
    Are they not in thy book?
Then my enemies will be turned back
    in the day when I call.
    This I know, that God is for me.
In God, whose word I praise,
    in the Lord, whose word I praise,
in God I trust without a fear.
    What can man do to me?
My vows to thee I must perform, O God;
    I will render thank offerings to thee.
For thou hast delivered my soul from death,
    yea, my feet from falling,
that I may walk before God
    in the light of life.
    (Psalm 56)

The Best Death Ever—Eva

> Watch therefore, for you do not know on what day your Lord
> is coming. But know this, that if the householder had known
> in what part of the night the thief was coming, he would have
> watched and would not have let his house be broken into.
> Therefore you also must be ready; for the Son of man is com-
> ing at an hour you do not expect.
>
> Matthew 24:42–44

In the petition for a painless, blameless, peaceful death, we are
essentially praying for a "good death." Throughout this book, I
will sprinkle in some stories of people for whom this petition came
true. Obviously, many deaths are tragic, drawn out, painful, or
sudden. But this story is about a sudden death that I think was
really a miracle. It certainly was the best death I have been privileged to witness.

Eva was a wonderful lady, a member of the Holy Trinity Greek
Orthodox Church in Asheville, where I was privileged to serve
from 2000 to 2004. She was 77 years old. And she was also a dear
friend. In fact, in 2004 my wife Lisa and I had made plans to get
together with her the Saturday after Pascha (Easter) to plant flowers in her yard.

On Holy Wednesday of that year, Eva was the last person to get anointed with holy unction. In fact, she remarked to me, "I'm glad I got to be last tonight so that we can chat for a few minutes." Our conversation wasn't particularly memorable; in fact, I remember only that we talked together on what would turn out to be her last full day on earth.

Remember Me, O Lord

On Holy Thursday evening, she attended the lengthy service of the twelve Gospel readings. She sat in her usual seat in the back pew on the right side, closest to the center aisle. After the procession of the crucified Christ, people came up row by row to venerate the cross as we continued the service. At some point after the procession, I walked down the center aisle with the censer. As I came to the back and censed the pew where Eva was, she did something unusual: Instead of bowing or making the sign of the cross, as is the Orthodox custom, she waved at me. I thought that was odd. I moved on to cense the narthex, and I looked through the glass partition separating it from the nave and saw Eva through the glass. She appeared to have a halo around her head—also something odd that I filed in my mind.

When people come up to venerate the cross during the service, I always tell them to stand or kneel and offer the prayer, "Remember me, O Lord, when You come into Your Kingdom."[9] The repentant thief said this to Christ, who answered him, "Truly I say to you, today you will be with me in Paradise" (Luke 23:43).

A few minutes after I had finished censing the church, Eva came up to venerate the cross. I was later told that she waved to people as

---

9   The actual verse of Scripture is, "Jesus, remember me when you come into your kingdom" (Luke 23:42).

she made her way up the aisle. She knelt in front of the cross, offered her prayer, and went back to her seat.

Eva sat down and had a massive heart attack. No trauma, no loud cry—she just fell over and stopped breathing.

The ushers came into the altar to tell me that someone was in medical distress, and they were calling 911. I asked, "Is it Eva?" because then I knew why she had waved to me. The service continued, the paramedics came, and I went to the back of the church briefly to anoint her with holy unction.

When the service concluded, they were still working on Eva. Rather than asking people to leave, I invited everyone to come up to front of the church. We knelt around the cross—150 of us—and sang hymns and offered prayers. After the paramedics took Eva's body out of the church, I followed them to the hospital, where she was pronounced dead on arrival. The paramedics had actually never found a pulse; she had most likely passed away in the church.

I stayed at the hospital for a few hours then returned with Eva's great-niece to the church to retrieve Eva's car. Her great-niece, a close friend, asked me to drive Eva's car back to her house, and she followed me in my car. I remember sitting down in Eva's car at 2 a.m. on Good Friday morning. I turned on the ignition, and her radio station came on. I saw a card with a reminder about her dentist appointment for the following day. The experience was surreal. Who parks their car at church and thinks, "The next person who drives the car will be my priest, because I will be dead"? Probably no one. Probably no one has ever had that thought in the history of the world!

I didn't get much sleep that night, nor did anyone else who witnessed what had happened. On Good Friday morning, I went to church for the Royal Hours, a service normally only attended by a few people, and was shocked to see the parish almost full, as it had been the night before. It seems that no one got any sleep, no one could go to work, and no one felt that they could do anything but go to church.

Our Good Friday adult retreat turned into a large group counseling session. I told people, "We didn't have a tragedy in our church last night; we had a miracle. A hundred and fifty people came up to the cross and said, 'Lord, remember me in Your Kingdom.' And to one He answered, 'Today you are with Me in Paradise.' If you wanted to pick a way to die, what better way than in church, surrounded by friends, with your last words being 'Lord, remember me in Your Kingdom,' and dying at the same hour that we commemorate the death of our Lord?"

Celebrating Eva's Resurrection Together

The Tuesday after Easter, the Orthodox Church celebrates the feast of Ss. Nicholas, Raphael, and Irene. Eva's funeral was held on that Tuesday in 2004. In a Liturgy that normally is not well attended, that year we had a packed church. The choir sang, and it was like the Resurrection service all over again. Again it seemed that no one could go to work; we all wanted closure with the woman we knew as a friend and who died in front of us. After the Liturgy, I went outside to escort the casket. As I entered the church, everyone stood up and sang "Christos anesti! Christ is risen!" As is the custom during Bright Week, we chanted the hymn ten times, with the verses from Psalm 68, which happens to be one of my favorite psalms.

After the first couple of repetitions of "Christos Anesti," I stopped and mentioned this is what it must sound like when someone goes to heaven—a choir of angels singing "Christos anesti!" and welcoming the new arrival. I turned toward the casket, holding the censer and my paschal candle, and intoned the verse, "Let God arise, let his enemies be scattered; / let those who hate him flee before him!" (Ps.

68:1), a verse of triumph and victory for God's people. I looked at Eva, and then I looked up and saw the empty cross behind the altar.[10] I felt not merely joy—I felt euphoria, ecstasy—and this remains one of the happiest moments of my life. We serve a God who rules over all, even over death, and He provided a miracle for a wonderful lady, a dear friend, and a dedicated Christian. Who could have lined up everything so perfectly, other than the perfect God?

The death of Eva was not a tragedy—it was a *miracle*, witnessed by the entire congregation at Holy Trinity Greek Orthodox Church in Asheville, North Carolina, on Holy Thursday evening of 2004. If one could say there was such a thing as a perfect death, this was it!

Remember thy word to thy servant,
    in which thou has made me hope.
This is my comfort in my affliction
    that thy promise gives me life.
Godless men utterly deride me,
    but I do not turn away from thy law.
When I think of thy ordinances from of old,
    I take comfort, O Lord.
Hot indignation seizes me because of the wicked,
    who forsake thy law.
Thy statutes have been my songs
    in the house of my pilgrimage.
I remember thy name in the night, O Lord,
    and keep thy law.
This blessing has fallen to me,
    that I have kept thy precepts.
(Psalm 119:49–56)

---

10 According to our tradition, the figure of Christ is removed for forty days as a sign of our Lord's victory over death.

Dealing with Tragedy

Why Do Bad Things Happen to Good People?

And the Lord said to Satan, "Have you considered my servant
Job, that there is none like him on the earth, a blameless and
upright man, who fears God and turns away from evil?" Then
Satan answered the Lord, "Does Job fear God for nought?
Hast thou not put a hedge about him and his house and all
that he has, on every side? Thou hast blessed the work of his
hands, and his possessions have increased in the land. But
put forth thy hand now, and touch all that he has, and he will
curse thee to thy face." And the Lord said to Satan,
"Behold, all that he has is in your power; only upon himself
do not put forth your hand." So Satan went forth from the
presence of the Lord.

Job 1:8–12

O f all the reflections in this book, this is the hardest one to write.
Most of us hope that we and our loved ones will live to be old.
Many people who are old hope for a quick and painless death. The
old usually view dying in one's sleep as a good way to go, even though
it is sudden. The people who will be left behind probably prefer death
that isn't sudden, where there is a chance to say good-bye.

But what about when death comes suddenly, or even tragically, to
someone who is young? We're not talking about someone who has

made a bad choice; we're talking about the otherwise healthy woman who has a sudden and fatal medical episode. Or the hard-working man who is killed in a car wreck on the way to work. Or the dedicated parent who dies in a freak accident, like slipping on a wet floor and hitting their head. I've known peak athletes who have died in their 30s and 40s—people who exercised every day and were extremely health conscious about eating. And I know people who are in their 70s and 80s who have abused their bodies, eating poorly and never exercising, yet somehow are still going. We've probably all had the experience of a close call in the car—a second earlier or later, we would have been in a crash. Why were we a split-second early or late when someone else was "on time" and was killed in a car wreck?

Trying to Understand God's Will

There is an intentional will of God. I believe that God is intentional about many things; for example, I believe He called me to be a priest. That calling was intentional.

There is also a permissive will of God. I don't believe that God intends for bad things to happen to people. However, He does permit them. Why? This has to do with free will. We touched on this topic earlier in the discussion of four causes of death (page 31), but let's look at our use of freedom again. For instance, if I'm talking to someone, I have a choice to treat them kindly or treat them unkindly. Let's say that I want to hit a person I am talking to. If I swing my arm at them and God stops my arm, that would be a miracle. God would stop a "law of nature" and do something extraordinary. But if God stops me every time I aim my fist at someone, then He's taken away my free will. I can no longer choose between being kind and unkind. And God usually does not take away our free will.

The questions for which there are no satisfactory answers (at least ones that I've discovered) are: Why does God perform a miracle in some instances and not in others? Why does God prevent certain things from happening, but in other cases He allows them? I do not have an answer for these.

I've had to bury several children who died when they were only days or months old. Why did God bring them into the world if they were only going to live a short time? Why did a mother get pregnant at all if her baby was destined to only live a few hours or days? Again, there are no answers to these questions. James 1:17 says, "Every good endowment and every perfect gift is from above, coming down from the Father of lights." If every good and perfect gift is from God, it would stand to reason that the opposite would also hold true—if it is not good, it is not from God. For instance, a headache is not good. If I have a headache, the source could be me—I didn't sleep enough, or I'm not hydrated. The source could be someone else—someone hit me in the head. The source could be the fallen natural world—too much sun. Or the source could be the "equal sharer in an imperfect nature" that I referenced before—the fallen world and its polluted air, water, and gene pools that will get each of us in some way.

Four Tough Questions

There are four questions I have reflected on each time I've ministered to people impacted by tragedy:

+ **"Why?"** Because of our bad choice, someone else's bad choice, a disaster of nature, equal sharers of an imperfect nature, and sometimes . . . there is no answer.
+ **"What if?"** This is where people second-guess decisions— fundamental ones like "Why did we have children?" or "Why did I do this or not do this?" The best answer to this question is, "'What if' is a bad question. Don't ask it." What-ifs will drive us crazy, make us feel guilty, and won't let us move on.

The constant replaying and wondering what could have been done differently, or looking back at forks in the road and wondering what would have happened had we chosen to follow a different path, will leave us sad, guilty, and despondent. "What if" is a natural question, but it is not really worth asking.

+ **"Where is God?"** People wonder where God was on 9/11. Why didn't God take over those planes from the terrorists? Why did God permit that? The simple answer is that bad people did a bad thing that day, and God doesn't stop people from doing bad things (most of the time) because He gave us free will, and free will can be used for destruction.

God is in the good. If something is not good, it is not from God. There were many stories of heroism from that day, and God was in every one of them. Good things have come out of 9/11, and God has been in every one of them. Again, I write this with humility. No one in my family was killed or hurt on that day. When the attacks happened, I felt pain as an American, not as someone close to a victim.

+ **"What now?"** I was going through a rough time when I was 19 years old and would ask myself, "Why do bad things keep happening to me?" I needed some serious surgery on my right elbow from an injury that effectively ended my participation in competitive sports. Now many decades past that, I realize that the operation was just a blip in my life, a tough time that I was able to get through. But back then, it was like my whole world was falling apart. I started to have some self-destructive thoughts—yes, most people have them at some point in life.[11]

I knew I needed some help, so I went and saw my priest and actually had my first confession at age 19. Our conversation

---

11   Such thoughts are not a problem unless they are constant, or there is a concern that you'll move past thoughts to self-destructive actions.

was one of the most impactful of my life. He told me one thing that I have taken to heart since that day. He said, "Don't be a victim. Be a survivor. God doesn't want victims; He wants survivors." I have tried to take a survivor mentality into my challenges—that whatever life throws me, I will somehow survive. For those who have dealt with tragedy, that's the best advice I could give. Find a way to survive. An elderly priest once told me that if someone is missing their pinky, they can find a way to cope with it. However, each time they look at their hand, they will realize something is missing. There are some tragedies in life that can make us think we can never recover from them or overcome. "Managing" and "enduring" become the operative ideas in how to move on from tragedy. At the end of life, when we are lying on our death bed, our past tragedies honestly won't matter. What will matter is whether we found a way to survive them.

Support in Times of Tragic Loss

Recall the Parable of the Talents in Matthew 25:14–30. The master entrusted to each of his servants a different amount of talents. And he expected a different result from each—in other words, a good return on His investment. From the one who received five, he expected five more. From the one who received two, he expected two more. I believe that for those of us whose lives have gone consistently well, God expects more from us. To the life beset by tragedy, God expects survival. He expects perseverance, getting through the remainder of our life while still remaining faithful to Him, following His commandments, and making the most we can with the talents and opportunities we still have in front of us.

Here are a few helpful hints in supporting people who have suffered tragic losses.

1. **Be present.** This is the most important hint. You don't have to say much. Just be there for those who are suffering. Rick Warren, the well-known Protestant pastor whose son died by suicide, is quoted as saying, "In deep pain, people don't need logic, advice, encouragement, or even Scripture. They just need you to show up and shut up."[12] I was encouraged as a young priest to have a "ministry of presence"—to be present without trying to come up with answers. Sometimes there are no answers, and whatever answers there may be, the time immediately after a loss is not the appropriate time to share them.

2. **Don't set a time limit on grief.** Many people heal at a funeral. But the relatives in tragedies need more time to heal. Parents who have lost children may cry the rest of their lives. And it is important that we give them space for their grief, that they don't feel that the clock is ticking when they talk about their child or their loss. Children who have lost parents at a young age also might need to grieve years later. For instance, a child at age 5 who loses a parent may grieve a little bit at graduation or a wedding—a life event when a parent is particularly missed. And they need to be allowed to do that.

3. **Let the person who has suffered tragedy lead the conversation.** Be sensitive to their mood, especially in the immediate aftermath. If they want to keep the conversation lighthearted, don't bring up heavy subjects. If they need to go deep and heavy, help them process their feelings. When they seem to need a break, try to offer something of a distraction. If they are grieving deeply and intensely, remind them to take deep breaths. Encourage tears. A person will need to cry a certain number of tears in the grieving process, and telling them not to cry just puts off what eventually needs to come out.

---

12 This saying is widely quoted, but the source is difficult to find.

There are no neat, tidy answers for life's tragedies. I have simply shared some thoughts that I have had over the years for dealing with pain, and they help me make sense of them. When tragedy happens to you, focus on being a survivor, not a victim. When tragedy happens to someone else, be present, and don't try to have any answers.

The LORD is my portion;
   I promise to keep thy words.
I entreat thy favor with all my heart;
   be gracious to me according to thy promise.
When I think of thy ways,
   I turn my feet to thy testimonies;
I hasten and do not delay
   to keep thy commandments.
Though the cords of the wicked ensnare me,
   I do not forget thy law.
At midnight I rise to praise thee,
   because of thy righteous ordinances.
I am a companion of all who fear thee,
   of those who keep thy precepts.
The earth, O LORD, is full of thy steadfast love;
   teach me thy statutes!
(Psalm 119:57–64)

It Doesn't Happen Here—Except, It Does

Then they cried to the LORD in their trouble, / and he delivered them from their distress;
he brought them out of darkness and gloom, / and broke their
bonds asunder.
Let them thank the LORD for his steadfast love, / for his wonderful works to the sons of men!

Psalm 107:13–15

I have always liked history. I remember as a young boy of ten years old watching a TV miniseries in 1982 called *Blood and Honor*. It was about the rise of the Hitler Youth in pre-World War II Germany. In a small town, Jewish families and German families grew up side by side. Kids went to school together, played together, and their parents were friends. When the Nazis came to power, word came to this small town that in the big cities, people were turning against each other, with Germans persecuting Jews. In this small town, the mother in a Jewish family said to her husband that maybe it would be a good idea for them to leave and go somewhere else before these things started to happen where they lived. He responded that it couldn't happen here. Except that it did. Eventually the persecution of the Jews happened in every town in Germany.

I currently live in Tampa, Florida. We are a good-sized city, but we are not New York or Los Angeles. We think of those places as big cities with big-city problems. Smaller towns think Tampa is a big city, with big-city problems. As a Greek American, my culture is a very small percentage of the United States population. When we think of societal problems, we think that they belong to other cultures—to bigger ethnic populations.

Except that they don't. Deep problems happen in every town and every ethnic group. And we can't pretend that they don't.

We Need to Talk About the Difficult Things

In more than twenty-five years of ministry, I have buried victims of suicide, homicide, and drug overdoses. I know that our community is not immune. Yet we are very hesitant to talk about these subjects. Just because someone is Greek, or Orthodox, or has a college degree, a good job, comes from a good family, or even is in church every Sunday does not mean that they are immune from family tragedies and personal struggles. At some point, just about all of us will know a victim of suicide, for example. No community is immune.

If we are really honest, we are all addicted to sin. We sin all the time; we can't stop. And sin, while a spiritual illness, is also a kind of mental illness because it takes root in the mind, and the mind is not able to stop it. We all need to protect ourselves mentally and spiritually. And this would be greatly aided if we could talk about these things. I think we can all do a better job of taking away the stigma of struggling with mental illness or addiction. I'm not ashamed to say that I have seen a therapist for years, yet some people stigmatize those who participate in any kind of therapy.

There should be no stigma to weakness and struggle. In our human condition, no one is perfect, and no one escapes difficulty. Some people are afraid to admit any weaknesses and vulnerabilities, not only out of embarrassment but out of fear; others think that real Christians always are victorious, or that to admit weakness somehow shows a lack of faith. Yet St. Paul freely admitted his own weaknesses. For those of us who struggle (and that means everyone), his words in 2 Corinthians 12:7–9 are some of the most encouraging and validating thoughts expressed in Scripture:

> And to keep me from being too elated by the abundance of revelations, a thorn was given me in the flesh, a messenger of Satan, to harass me, to keep me from being too elated. Three times I besought the Lord about this, that it should leave me; but he said to me, "My grace is sufficient for you, for my power is made perfect in weakness." I will all the more gladly boast of my weaknesses, that the power of Christ may rest upon me.

Facing Suicide

I've spoken to a few survivors of suicide attempts, and one thing I've come to understand is that some people who die by suicide are not necessarily at rock bottom; they are working their way back up and just can't see the light. For instance, a student who struggles with grades—who perhaps has a C- average—feels like a failure. And then he brings up his average to a B- and becomes despondent because he still sees how far he has to go, rather than how far he has come.

To make an analogy, if someone is standing in the sunlight and then begins to descend a spiral staircase below ground, at ten steps down they can still see light. At twenty steps they are in total darkness. Let's say that when they hit the bottom they are forty steps down. They start to come back, and they expend the energy to climb up twenty stairs. But rather than feeling a sense of accomplishment, they are still in darkness. They think they will never be in the light again, and they give up. But with just a little encouragement, they might have kept climbing. In the same way, those who die by suicide are not necessarily at rock bottom. Some are on the way back up but don't feel like it because it is still so dark.

I know situations where people have died by suicide and those around them said, "No one saw that coming." This is why we need to be careful and keep watch over those around us.

I also know of people who have died by suicide and others said, "We all saw that coming." This begs the question, "If everyone saw it coming, why didn't anyone do anything about it?"

Empathy and Nonjudgment

People die from massive heart attacks all the time, and there is no stigma associated with this. It's fair to say that the cause of suicide is a "massive brain attack," where all hope and reason leave and the person does something unthinkable—usually something out of character. It is also fair to say that someone "died from suicide" rather than "committed suicide." People die from heart disease all the time, and many die from "death by donut" because they eat so poorly. But they don't "commit a heart attack."

Careless words can assign blame. People who lose loved ones to suicide, drug addiction, and foul play are often beset with guilt and shame. They do not need any more. The best thing we can do is to be present, without judgment, without gossiping about it. Just be present.

Regarding these kinds of death, we need more awareness. We need to talk about these things more. We need to pay attention to those around us, to listen for clues that people so often leave yet just aren't picked up on. We need more empathy rather than judgment for loved ones left behind. The world has enough shame. It doesn't need more. And we need to stop being ignorant, pretending that these kinds of things do not happen in our community, because they do. I'm reminded of the verse in Genesis 4:9, after Cain killed his brother, Abel. "The LORD said to Cain, 'Where is Abel your brother?' He said, 'I do not know; am I my brother's keeper?'" The answer is, Yes, we are!

We all need to be more proactive and empathetic regarding the issues of suicide, drug addiction, and homicide. They happen every-where. Including right here.

> As a hart longs for flowing streams,
>> so longs my soul for thee, O God.
> My soul thirsts for God,
>> for the living God.
> When shall I come and behold the face of God?
>> My tears have been my food
> day and night,
>> while men say to me continually,
> "Where is your God?"

> These things I remember,
>> as I pour out my soul:
> how I went with the throng,
>> and led them in procession to the house of God,
> with glad shouts and songs of thanksgiving,
>> a multitude keeping festival.
> Why are you cast down, O my soul,
>> and why are you disquieted within me?
> Hope in God; for I shall again praise him,
>> my help and my God.

> My soul is cast down within me,
>> therefore I remember thee
> from the land of Jordan and of Hermon,
>> from Mount Mizar.

Deep calls to deep
  at the thunder of thy cataracts;
all thy waves and thy billows
  have gone over me.
By day the LORD commands his steadfast love;
  and at night his song is with me,
  a prayer to the God of my life.

I say to God, my rock:
  "Why hast thou forgotten me?
Why go I mourning
  because of the oppression of the enemy?"
As with a deadly wound in my body,
  my adversaries taunt me,
while they say to me continually,
  "Where is your God?"

Why are you cast down, O my soul,
  and why are you disquieted within me?
Hope in God; for I shall again praise him,
  my help and my God.
(Psalm 42)

The Worst Way to Die

He who believes in him is not condemned; he who does not believe is condemned already, because he has not believed in the name of the only Son of God.

John 3:18

One of my favorite movies is *Vacation*, starring Chevy Chase. In a great scene, Aunt Edna, a rude old woman who tags along on the Griswald family's vacation across America, dies. They put her on the patio of Cousin Normie's house and cover her with a blanket and an umbrella because it's raining. In a hurry to move along on the vacation, Clark (Chevy Chase's character) rushes to leave. Clark's wife, who is related to Aunt Edna, insists that he "say something." So Clark gathers the family and offers a most irreverent prayer: "O God, ease our suffering in this, our moment of great despair. Yea, admit this good and decent woman into Thine arms and the flock in Thine heavenly area up there. And Moab he laidest down behind the land of the Canaanites. And yea, though the Hindus speak of karma—I implore You, give her a break."[13]

---

13   From transcript of *National Lampoon's Vacation* (Warner Bros., 1983), script
-o-rama.com/movie_scripts/v/vacation-script-transcript-chevy-chase.html.

Hospital Visits with Strangers

This scene from *Vacation* plays through my mind every so often when I go to the hospital to minister to someone I don't know who is dying. The scene plays out often enough that it merits mention in this book on a painless, blameless, Christian end to our lives. I receive a call from a hospital asking "for a Greek priest" to visit someone's yiayia (grandmother) who is dying. I will of course go to the hospital and minister to the patient and the family because Christian love dictates so.

Many times, by this point the patient is unresponsive. And the family will say something like, "Do that thing you do so that Yiayia will go to heaven"—as if I have some kind of mystical power to send someone to heaven. They will insist that I give Yiayia Holy Communion, as if it is some kind of magic elixir that will make up for the fact that Yiayia hasn't been in church for years, maybe even decades. In order to receive Holy Communion, the communicant must meet many "requirements," if you will, the first of which is faith in Jesus Christ. On a practical level, one must voluntarily agree to receive Holy Communion—it is not imposed on someone. And they must be able to consume the Communion—that is, they need to be able to swallow.[14]

I have experienced numerous instances throughout my ministry when I went to the hospital to visit someone who stopped coming to church years before—usually because they were angry with

---

14 One fascinating thing that often happens with people who have dementia is that they won't recognize a person or remember a name, but when they hear a hymn being sung, they will do something that indicates they understand on some level what is going on. Some people who have had strokes and can no longer talk will sing a hymn with me and then become silent again. Some great advice I received when I was a new priest was, "Always sing when you visit someone, especially someone with cognitive impairment. It unlocks part of their brain and takes them back to younger years." This advice is good for people who aren't priests, too.

someone—or I visited someone who never attended church. The conversation usually goes something like this:

I ask, "Is there anything you would like to talk about regarding your faith?"

They answer, "How are you, Father?"

"We're not here to talk about me, we're here to talk about you."

They continue with something like, "How are your wife and your son? Are you happy in this community?"

"Sir/Ma'am," I say, "I'm here because you are dying, probably tonight. I'm here to see if there is anything you want to talk about regarding your faith—if you are scared, if you are ready to meet the Lord, if there is anything you want to talk about before you pass away."

"I'm good, Father."

I try again. "You haven't been in church in years. I'm not asking you to have this conversation with me; I'm *begging* you to have it."

And the reply is often: "I'm all good."

These are some of the most heartbreaking moments of ministry, when people won't talk about their faith at the very end. I'm always sad when I walk away from visits like this.

Situations like the one with Yiayia or the person who won't talk about God when they are dying happen all the time. People give no thought to faith, and at the end they either remain apathetic or cry out in desperation for me to do something to make up for all the years of indifference. People have actually said to me many times over the years, "You understand, Father, I've been busy my whole life. I was always working, so I never came to church. You understand, right?" And I think, "It's not me that sits on the judgment seat; you don't have to convince me."

One thing we should all understand is that God will decide who enters His Kingdom and who does not. No one—not even the priest—has the power to declare someone is going or not going to heaven. That decision rests with the Lord and with Him alone. It is very sad to me, however, when people pass away without much sense of the Lord, or desire to know Him; they have spent no time learning about Him, worshiping Him, or telling others about Him. I don't know the heart of people who don't worship, but I would imagine that those who never attend church are probably not spending a whole lot of time praying, reading the Bible, repenting, or encouraging others to do the same.

The saddest deaths are these final moments of desperation or indifference. When I think of the worst possible way to die, I don't think of a disfiguring accident or a painful illness. I think the worst way to die is without faith in Christ—without even giving thought to the Faith. Because at the end of life, faith is all that will matter. It is the only thing we can take with us.

> Thou hast dealt well with thy servant,
>   O Lord, according to thy word.
> Teach me good judgment and knowledge,
>   for I believe in thy commandments.
> Before I was afflicted I went astray;
>   but now I keep thy word.
> Thou art good and doest good;
>   teach me thy statutes.
> The godless besmear me with lies,
>   but with my whole heart I keep thy precepts;
> their heart is gross like fat,
>   but I delight in thy law.
> It is good for me that I was afflicted,
>   that I might learn thy statutes.
> The law of thy mouth is better to me
>   than thousands of gold and silver pieces.
> (Psalm 119:65–72)

The Woman Who Had Nothing, and Yet Had Everything—Stavroula

> She who is a real widow, and is left all alone, has set her hope on God and continues in supplications and prayers night and day.
>
> 1 Timothy 5:5

When someone close to us dies, we feel sad, we cry, we mourn, we remember, we tell stories about them to keep their memory fresh in our minds. Can you imagine if someone died and no one felt sad, no one cried, no one came, and no one remembered?

In 2004, on Holy Monday in the parish in Asheville, North Carolina, where I was serving at the time, one such person died. I feel compelled to share her story because no one else in the world is talking about her today.

Alone in the World

On that day at 5:15 a.m., I received a called from a health care center saying that a woman named Stavroula (Stella) Anthopoulos had passed away. The person on the phone told me that not only was I listed on her chart as her priest but also as her next of kin. And then I heard the standard words: "If you don't want to claim her, she will be cremated and placed in an unmarked grave at a local cemetery." And completely forgotten.

Stavroula was born in Greece. At one point she was married, and later her husband abandoned her. She had a son, and he too abandoned her. She found herself living on a small pension in Asheville, North Carolina. Her money began to run out, and her health took a turn downward. Because she waited too long to have cataracts removed, she lost her eyesight. With nowhere to turn, she became a ward of the state of North Carolina. She lived in a nursing home for the last seven years of her life. She was blind—she couldn't see to read, walk, or watch TV. She couldn't speak English, and so she often went days without talking to anyone. She was all alone in the world.

The anniversary of my ordination to the priesthood is May 15. I have always celebrated Liturgy on my anniversary and have always made a point of visiting someone in a hospital to mark that day each year. I had recently arrived in Asheville in May 2000, and my anniversary came. I asked if anyone was in the hospital, and fortunately, the answer was no. But a lady named Mary Pappas told me about Stavroula—that she was alone in a nursing home and that Mary was her only visitor. That day, Mary and I went to visit Stavroula.

Faithfulness in Solitude

For four years, Mary Pappas and I visited Stella faithfully at least seven or eight times a year: for Christmas, Epiphany, Holy Week, and to sing "Christ is Risen" after Pascha; on August 15, the Dormition of the Virgin Mary and also Mary's nameday; and for Stavroula's nameday on September 14 (my nameday also). And every year on May 15, the anniversary of my ordination to the priesthood, I would always go and spend time with Stavroula after the Liturgy. I could gather that she must have been a very faithful attendee at church services at some point in her life.

It's hard to know how to pray with someone who is so ill yet is not about to die. It didn't seem right to pray for her to get better or to pray for a peaceful ending either. So, we would pray for strength, and then we would sing hymns, and this would pull her out of her sometimes very withdrawn mood. She knew the words to all the hymns, which always amazed me. Even if she seemed unresponsive to our greeting, as soon as she heard singing, she would make her cross and sing with us.

Our conversations were short but memorable. I remember one time she told me she had a dream and that she saw me in the dream celebrating the Liturgy. I asked her what I looked like, because she was blind and had never actually seen me. She said I had medium-length blond hair, so she made me look better than I actually look. One time I asked if she wanted to receive Communion, and she said she had to wash her hands first, because she was dirty. After we washed and dried her hands, she received Communion.

Her humility humbled me. Once Mary and I went to visit Stavroula, and she was praying. She didn't see or hear us come in, and I motioned to Mary that we should be quiet and wait for her to finish her prayer. She asked in her prayer if "God could send Father and Mary" because she wanted to see us. We said, "Here we are, Stavroula." She smiled and said, "That's the quickest I've ever had a prayer answered."

A few months before Stella died, she asked me to talk to her about what heaven is like. The week before she died on a Friday afternoon, she did an interesting thing. On every visit we would sing hymns from that liturgical period in the church year, and so on that Friday before Palm Sunday, we sang hymns from Lent and Holy Week. She sang with us "Victorious Lady" (*Ti Upermacho*) and the hymn of Palm Sunday evening, "Behold the Bridegroom Comes." She then abruptly stopped singing as we sang the hymns of Holy Week. At the time, we couldn't figure out why.

Shortly after we left, she suffered a massive stroke, and I was told she was going to die very soon. I thought that maybe she stopped singing the hymns because she was not going to be alive during Holy Week. Sure enough, she passed away Holy Monday morning, after we had sung the hymn of Palm Sunday night at church.

God's Divine Hand Was Certainly Present

I've never cried so much at a funeral as I did when I buried Stavroula. Perhaps that is because no one else in the world was crying for her, so God brought tears to my eyes. I remember doing all the arrangements for her funeral. I did not pay to have her embalmed, I got the least expensive casket and bought flowers from the market, and it still cost me $6,000.

About a month later, I mentioned to my congregation that I needed help paying off my credit card bill from the funeral. That night, at a wedding, a guest came up to me at the reception and said that he had been in church and heard about what I did for Stavroula. He handed me an envelope and told me to open it after I left the wedding reception. In the car, I opened the envelope and found $6,000 in cash. I went back in and asked the man his name, because I didn't know him. He said, "My name is Michael, like the Archangel, and that's all you need to know."

God's sense of timing is perfect. During my last year in Asheville, Holy Monday was April 5. That put Stavroula's forty-day memorial on my anniversary, May 15. So, again I celebrated my name-day Liturgy and visited Stavroula.

The only empty spot in the Greek section of the cemetery happened to be next to Mary Pappas, and Stavroula is buried there. On my last Sunday in Asheville, we dedicated her tombstone, which I designed. It reads, "Behold the Bridegroom Comes, in the middle of the night, and blessed is the servant He shall find patiently waiting."

Mary Pappas passed away in 2021 and is buried next to Stavroula. Mary and I were Stavroula's "family," and now that Mary is gone, I'm the only one left who talks about Stavroula, which is why she is included in this book.

I didn't know Stavroula in her healthy life. I don't know what she did. I'm sure she had her joys and her sorrows, her triumphs and her mistakes. What I do know is that she'd led a very difficult existence for many years. She couldn't see, watch TV, or read; she had difficulty communicating because her English wasn't very good; she was surrounded by strangers in a strange place, and she was grateful for their love and care. While people were going about their lives, she was all alone, unable to do much of anything but sit and pray. And yet, she was so happy to pray, eager to meet the Lord, that she filled her days praying by herself.

She remembered so many of the hymns of our church, and as her eyes lost sight of the world and her mind began to lose much of its abilities and knowledge, her heart always remembered God. She got frustrated often, and told us so, but she never lost faith. She truly was an example of what St. Paul writes about in the Epistle to the Corinthians (2 Cor. 6:10), as a person "having nothing, and yet possessing everything."

I pray that her eyes have now been reopened to see the glory of God in heaven. While I was fortunate to have seen her for four years, I can only hope that I one day find myself in heaven so that she can see me.

Memory eternal, Stavroula!

Incline thy ear, O LORD, and answer me,
    for I am poor and needy.
Preserve my life for I am godly;
    save thy servant who trusts in thee.
Thou art my God; be gracious to me, O LORD,

for to thee do I cry all the day.
Gladden the soul of thy servant,
    for to thee, O Lord, do I lift up my soul.
For thou, O Lord, art good and forgiving,
    abounding in steadfast love to all who call on thee.
Give ear, O Lord, to my prayer;
    hearken to my cry of supplication.
In the day of my trouble I call on thee,
    for thou dost answer me.

There is none like thee among the gods, O Lord,
    nor are there any works like thine.
All the nations thou has made shall come
    and bow down before thee, O Lord,
    and shall glorify thy name.
For thou art great and doest wondrous things,
    thou alone art God.
Teach me thy way, O Lord,
    that I may walk in thy truth;
    unite my heart to fear thy name.
I give thanks to thee, O Lord my God, with my whole heart,
    and I will glorify thy name forever.
For great is thy steadfast love toward me;
thou has delivered my soul from the depths of Sheol.

O God, insolent men have risen against me;
    a band of ruthless men seek my life,
    and they do not set thee before them.
But thou, O Lord, art a God merciful and gracious,
    slow to anger and abounding in steadfast love and
    faithfulness.

Turn to me and take pity on me;
    give thy strength to thy servant,
    and save the son of thy handmaid.
Show me a sign of thy favor,
    that those who hate me may see and be put to shame,
    because thou, Lord, hast helped me and comforted me.
(Psalm 86)

Getting Ready

I'm Afraid to Die—Dad

Since therefore the children share in flesh and blood, he himself likewise partook of the same nature, that through death
he might destroy him who has the power of death, that is, the
devil, and deliver all those who through fear of death were
subject to lifelong bondage.

Hebrews 2:14–15

In over twenty-five years as a priest, I have participated in the
deaths and/or funerals of more than three hundred people. One
of my motivations for this book is to share some of the good experiences while also touching on a few of the harder ones. This reflection is more personal, because it involves the death of my dad and
the lessons—good and bad—that I took away from it. It will also
be a little bit longer than the other chapters. There is a lot to my
dad's story, but I'm not going to reflect on his life or what kind of dad
he was. He had a good life and was a good dad. These are thoughts
about the end of his life.

A Lifelong Fear of Death

First of all, Dad had a lifelong fear of death. He didn't want to talk
about it; he didn't want to think about life insurance or a will or

anything like that. He took it very hard when family or friends died. Second, Dad was a devout Orthodox Christian. He sang in the choir every Sunday until a few weeks before his death. He was always in church. He knew many verses of Scripture, and the pages of his Bible and prayer book were worn thin from use. Dad loved going to church. He lit a candle in front of our icons at home every morning, without fail.

Dad also wasn't as faithful about going to the doctor as he should have been. He survived prostate cancer in his 60s. However, he didn't have a colonoscopy until he was 76, when he was diagnosed with stage-four colon cancer.

So, **Lesson One** from my Dad: If you are over 50, get a colonoscopy. No one should die from this disease.

Dad lived with colon cancer for about thirty months, which is twelve months longer than the doctors estimated. He was definitely a fighter. And most of that time was actually a good time: He went on living, and he assumed he would beat the cancer.

More Lessons from My Dad's Death

In May 2014, Dad was in the hospital, and his health was starting to deteriorate. My brother told me that I should come home to Los Angeles. The end was coming, and if I wanted to see Dad while he was still aware and responsive, now was the time to visit. I told Dad I was coming home, and he got upset with me.

"The doctors are all wrong," he said. "I will be fine." I told him that I wanted to come and see him despite his objections.

I flew home on a Wednesday, and Dad was released from the hospital while I was en route. So I saw him at home. The next day happened to be the Feast of the Ascension, and I asked Dad if he wanted to go to church. He said he did, but he wanted to go to a different Orthodox parish in the area because he didn't want his friends to know how sick he was. We went to church, he saw me celebrate the Divine Liturgy one last time, and I was able to give him Communion.

That night, he asked me if we could talk. He said, "Son, I think I am going to die, and I am afraid to die. Will you make me not afraid?"

I answered him, "Dad, I'll have this conversation with you if I can have it as a priest and not as your son."

He said, "Whatever makes you feel comfortable."

I asked him, "Dad, do you believe in God?"

"Yes, I believe in God."

"What do you believe about God?"

And he answered, "I'm not sure."

This was **Lesson Two**: Just because someone faithfully attends church doesn't mean that they understand the Faith. My dad went to church every Sunday, sang in the choir, did everything we hope our parishioners do, has one son who is a priest and the other who is a parish council president, and sat through many Holy Week services. Yet now, at the end of life, he not only was scared but also confused about what he actually believed.

This was a light-bulb moment for me as a priest. We need to do a better job of educating people about life and death. And from the non-priest perspective, the people need to be better students— investing the time, asking the questions, and having the tough conversations.

Fortunately, I had served as the director of our metropolis summer camp for many years, and one of my responsibilities was writing the curriculum. I told him, "Dad, you are in luck—our theme for summer camp this year is the Creed and what we believe. I was working on it on the plane ride over here."

So I got out the curriculum, and we went through the Creed. We talked about why we die and about how death is like graduating from college—some of the things we've discussed in this book. When we finished, he said, "Now I understand death, but how can I prepare?"

I asked him, "Have you ever gone for confession?" and explained what confession is. He said that he had never been. This is surprisingly common among many Orthodox Christians. Perhaps the sacrament isn't emphasized enough. I'm sure some priests shy away from teaching about confession, and many of the faithful either do not appreciate its importance or are too embarrassed to go. I think in my dad's instance, it was a case of ignorance. When I was growing up, our priests didn't teach about it. So, I suggested that we call a priest to come over to hear his confession.

He looked at me and said, "You are the priest. You said you are not my son tonight. You hear the confession."

That was super awkward. But I put on my stole and sat next to him on his right side, as I do for all the confessions I hear. I remember nothing of what he said because I never remember anything I hear in confession.[15] All I remember is that when we were done, he said to me, "Father"—he always called me Stavros, but in line with the theme of the night, he called me Father—"get on your knees next to me, and pray for me to die. Because if I die now, I am ready." And he added, "Stavros, thank you for making me not afraid to die. I wish I had had this conversation with you thirty years ago. I wouldn't have spent my senior years in fear of this. Son, I was so sad when you left for the priesthood and you didn't come home often. But this makes it all worth it. Your (younger) brother, Joe, was like my first-born

---

15 After my first confession, I went to see my priest a few months later and I thanked him for our conversation. He said, "I don't remember the conversation." I asked, "How can you not remember when it was so meaningful for me?" He said, "The grace of the Holy Spirit that comes upon you to wipe away your sins also comes on me and wipes away my memory of the conversation." I didn't really believe that until I became a priest and started hearing confessions. Several people over the years have mentioned that something I said was very impactful for them. And I repeat the same thing my priest said to me.

son—he helped take care of me throughout my life. And you, son—you came to take care of me in death."

It was the best conversation I had ever had with my dad. I asked him, "Do you want me to serve at your funeral or sit in the pews with Mom and Joe?"

He said, "I did not give you to the Church so you could sit in the pews and watch someone else do the funeral. You do the funeral, and make me look good. And please don't cry when you do it. Be the priest at my funeral."

We finished the conversation with me encouraging my dad to call his friends and let them come to the house to say their good-byes. I told him that these people had loved him his whole life, and they should have closure. He finally decided to tell his friends. He also signed a do-not-resuscitate (DNR) order and the papers for hospice so that he could die at home, which he did.

Lesson Three from my dad's death was: He found his salvation in the way he died. What do I mean by that? Two thousand years ago, if someone had walked up to Golgotha, they would have seen Jesus, a young man who lived His life doing good things—working miracles, teaching, hanging out with the downtrodden—being killed in horrific way. An observer might have wondered, "What was the point of killing this man in the most heinous way possible?" Two thousand years later, we know that what happened on Golgotha opened the gates of Paradise to billions of people who believe in Jesus Christ as the Son of God. Through His sacrifice they—we—have found purpose, meaning, and ultimately salvation.

For my dad, as he sat there in sweatpants wearing a catheter and in obvious discomfort, I wondered, "Why cancer? Why like this?" And the answer now, in retrospect, is that in his suffering, Dad found *his* salvation.

Many people throughout my ministry have said, "If I could have had one more conversation with my dad (or mom, or someone else who has passed away), there are so many things I wish I had said." I knew that trip home would be the last time I would see my dad, and I decided that when it was time to leave, I would say what I wanted to say. Then I wouldn't feel the regret so many people experience because they didn't get proper closure. I decided that right before I was going to leave for the airport, I would say good-bye to Dad in the living room where he was sitting. Then my brother would come in and sit with him. I would get up and not look back, and Dad wouldn't look out the window and see me drive away.

I asked my brother and my mom to give me some privacy with Dad, which they did. I told my dad that I loved him, I thanked him for being my dad, I offered a prayer for him, and we sang the hymn of St. Nicholas, his patron saint. And the last thing I did was get on my knees, like the figures of the Old Testament—Isaac, Jacob, Joseph, Joshua, and many others—and ask Dad to put his hand on my head and give me his blessing. The last thing he said to me was, *"Na ehis tin efhi mou"*—a Greek expression that means, "You have my blessing."

I kissed his hand, stood up, and left quietly. My brother came and sat with Dad. Both my dad and I had tears during this conversation, but we both felt at peace when it was done.

Lesson Four from my dad's death: Say what you want to say—a proper good-bye. Don't fight it all the way to the end.

Ready to Go

After our final visit together, I returned to Florida. Dad lived just over sixteen more days after our good-bye. We had a few more interesting conversations on the phone before he passed, and he shared with me that he had had two significant dreams. In one dream, he was running through the harbor of Chania, the city in Crete where he grew up. People were yelling at him to go and catch his boat because it was leaving. He thought the dream was odd, because he had never owned a boat. I told him I thought the dream was about him exiting this life and God coming for him, like a boat sailing out of the harbor in Crete—that Dad should run to the boat and get on it.

In the second dream, Dad told me that he was standing in front of the royal gates of the altar in the parish he attended, and our mom was standing apart from him. Someone was beckoning him to go through the gates, and he was arguing that only the clergy go through there. I told him that the royal gates represent the gates of heaven, and Mom was not dying now, so he should listen and go through them.

In my last conversations with my dad, he grunted a few words and didn't say anything much. However, I had already had my good-bye conversation with him, so these calls don't really count in my mind. I had experienced the conversation that really counted.

On Father's Day in 2014, my dad was somehow still clinging to life on the sixteenth day after our good-byes. I texted my mom during the Liturgy. I hardly ever do that; it's inappropriate to text in church, but I made an exception that day and asked my mom if Dad wanted me to come home again—if that's why he hadn't passed away yet. She said that Dad was watching the service on livestream, waiting for me to say the Creed. He also said he didn't want to die on Father's Day because he didn't want to ruin the day for us.

Mom told me later that Dad said the Creed aloud with me that Sunday. He never spoke another word after that. His last words were, "I look for the Resurrection of the dead and the life of the age to come. Amen."[16] After reciting the Creed, Dad closed his eyes and rested. He passed away shortly after 1:00 a.m. Pacific Time on Monday, June 16, 2014. Indeed, he had made it through Father's Day.

---

16   *Divine Liturgy of St. John Chrysostom* (2015), 47.

On the plane flight to California, I cried the entire way. I practiced his funeral in my head several times, and I cried each time. When I conducted the funeral for real a few days later, I didn't cry. Dad got his wish.

Dad was buried on June 20, 1979, on what would have been his seventieth birthday, which is also Joe's birthday. People told me I looked peaceful and content at Dad's funeral. I told them that his wish for that day was for me to be in the role of priest and not son. Something beautiful happens when I step in front of the altar with my vestments on. Most of the time I feel happy, peaceful, and content. And I certainly felt that at my dad's funeral. I did take a moment to be a son—I told the other clergy who were present that when we sang "Memory eternal" at the end, I would go and stand in the front row with my family. It was during that hymn that I shed a few tears.

In my last conversation with him, I asked my dad to visit me in my dreams once in a while so that I would know he is okay. About once a year I have the same dream about him: I'm at St. Anthony Greek Orthodox Church in Pasadena, my dad's parish, and I'm in the altar putting on my vestments to celebrate the Divine Liturgy. Dad comes hobbling up the right-side aisle, and I rush to greet him.

I say, "Dad, what are you doing here? You look terrible."

And he answers, "You told me to visit you once in a while to let you know that I'm okay."

"You don't look okay."

And he says, "I'm very happy where I am. God told me that when I go visit you, I have to have my old, tired body so I won't want to stay here with you. So, if you just do the service quick today, I want to go back, because I'm very happy where I am."

When I wake up from this dream, about once year, I'm always happy because he is happy.

Memory eternal, Dad!

Save me, O God, by thy name,
   and vindicate me by thy might.
Hear my prayer, O God;
   give ear to the words of my mouth.

For insolent men have risen against me,
   ruthless men seek my life;
   they do not set God before them.

Behold, God is my helper;
   the Lord is the upholder of my life.
He will requite my enemies with evil;
   in thy faithfulness put an end to them.

With a freewill offering I will sacrifice to thee;
   I will give thanks to thy name, O Lord, for it is good.
For thou hast delivered me from every trouble,
   and my eye has looked in triumph on my enemies.
(Psalm 54)

I'm Ready to Die—Fr. Basil

Who then is the faithful and wise servant, whom his master has set over his household, to give them their food at the proper time? Blessed is that servant whom his master when he comes will find so doing.

Matthew 24:45–46

Father Basil served as an Orthodox priest for over fifty years. In his retirement, he attended different parishes in the area and occasionally would worship at mine. By the time I met him, he was beyond the ability to be able to serve, as his health was poor.

One day his wife called and told me he wasn't doing well, and she asked about having the funeral at St. John in Tampa, where I serve. This was a little surprising, actually, since I didn't know him well and thought he was much closer to other priests and parishes than to me.

I asked her, "Does he have a file for what he wants at his funeral?" Many priests have a file where they have written down what vestments they want to be buried in, who should get their remaining vestments, and answers to other questions.

She answered, "He's very particular, just like you, and he knew you'd ask that question. That's why he wants you to take care of the arrangements."

I told her I was happy to do so.

A Final Confession

It was Saturday, December 2, 2006, when Fr. Basil's wife called and asked me to come visit him in the hospital. I arrived around 5:00 p.m., just before sunset. Father Basil's blood pressure was so low that even the medical personnel were amazed that he was still alive. After exchanging pleasantries, he said to me and to his family, "I have been at the bedside of countless people who were at the end of life these last fifty years. I always wondered what it would be like when it was my time. I always dreamed that I would have my family around me, and I would have a priest hear my last confession." With that, his family respectfully left the room.

I sat by his bedside and looked out the window as the sun was going down over Tampa Bay. I thought to myself, "This is the last time the sun will set on this man's life. I wonder what he will confess. Will he be bitter from all the wounds we take in ministry? Will he be anxious?"

In very weak voice, in a slow cadence, Fr. Basil began to speak: "I believe in one God, the Father Almighty, Creator of heaven and earth, and all things visible and invisible . . ." He was reciting the Creed. It took several minutes for him to get through it.

Initially I thought to myself, "What kind of confession is this? Where are his sins?" Then, as I heard the conviction in his very weak voice, I realized this man had been confessing his sins for his entire life. He had been repenting and making corrections. And now, at the moment of his death, as he was about to close his eyes to life in this world, he wanted to confess his faith, his belief and hope that he would open them again and see the Lord and a new life.

His final confession was not a confession of sin but a confession of faith, made possible because he had spent a lifetime repenting his sins.

He finished the Creed, reciting those words, "I look to the Resurrection of the dead and the life of the age to come. Amen."[17] Tears rolled down his cheeks. I could see a man of deep faith who had a profound hope in what was coming next. He was so tired and yet joyful.

He reached for my hand, looked at me, and said, "I'll see you in Paradise. Consider me good to go." This wasn't some arrogant or proud statement. He wasn't claiming Paradise for himself. He was saying that his whole life had been leading him up to this moment and that rather than being in fear of the unknown, he was ready to meet the Lord.

I offered a prayer for Fr. Basil, and his family came back into the room. I offered him Holy Communion. I took off my stole and placed it around Fr. Basil's neck. I put in his hand a small blessing cross I carry to hospitals. His family then came to receive his blessing—as their father, grandfather, husband, and priest.

I left the hospital shortly afterward and went home. I figured it would be just a matter of time before I got called back to the hospital, so I just stayed in my work clothes for a while. Around 11:00 p.m. I got tired and decided to go to sleep. As I was getting into bed, wondering why I hadn't gotten called back to the hospital, it dawned on me that Fr. Basil was going to die at the time of the Resurrection— after the Sabbath (Saturday) had passed and before the sun would rise on Sunday. I laid out a set of clothes next to the bed so I wouldn't have to fumble around the room if a call came in the middle of the night. Sure enough, the call came at 5:30 a.m. that Fr. Basil was passing. I drove to the hospital as the sun was about to rise.

Many years later, in November 2023, Fr. Basil's wife, Presbytera Loretta, also passed away. I visited her for what was our final time together. She remembered my final visit with her husband and she

---

17   *Divine Liturgy of St. John Chrysostom* (2015), 47.

asked if she could do the same. We said the Creed, she received Holy Communion, and a few days later, she passed.

Two Lessons from Fr. Basil

I have taken away two lessons from the death of Fr. Basil. **Lesson One:** When I have a sense that I am visiting someone for the last time, I always say the Creed. Sometimes the person will say it with me. Other times they are unconscious, and I hope that they are hearing it and saying it with me subconsciously. People often ask me the question, "What are the requirements to receive Holy Communion?" They get caught up with fasting, and they miss the most basic requirement, which is to believe in God. That is why at the Divine Liturgy we always recite the Creed—in order to confess our faith before we receive Holy Communion. Before we leave this life and meet the Lord, I think it is an important and beautiful thing to confess our faith.

Lesson Two I've taken away from the death of Fr. Basil is a greater understanding of the Sacrament of Confession. Confession is something we should be doing on a regular basis. It is important to have a relationship with a priest, known as a spiritual father, who will offer guidance for our spiritual lives, including how often we should go to confession. Confession affords us the opportunity to rid ourselves of shame, to correct our course through repentance, and to recommit ourselves to the Faith. If a person has been confessing and repenting throughout their lives, then the last confession really should be a confession of faith.

Confession of sins and confession of faith go hand in hand. A lifetime of confessing and repenting should lead to a confession of faith at the end that is filled with hope—and even joy.

Praise the LORD!
For it is good to sing praises to our God;

for he is gracious, and a song of praise is seemly.
The LORD builds up Jerusalem;
    he gathers the outcasts of Israel.
He heals the brokenhearted,
    and binds up their wounds.
He determines the number of the stars,
    he gives to all of them their names.
Great is our LORD, and abundant in power;
    his understanding is beyond measure.
The LORD lifts up the downtrodden,
    he casts the wicked to the ground.

Sing to the LORD with thanksgiving;
    make melody to our God upon the lyre!
He covers the heavens with clouds,
    he prepares rain for the earth,
    he makes grass grow upon the hills.
He gives to the beasts their food,
    and to the young ravens which cry.
His delight is not in the strength of the horse,
    nor his pleasure in the legs of a man;
but the LORD takes pleasure in those who fear him,
    in those who hope in his steadfast love.

Praise the LORD, O Jerusalem!
    Praise your God, O Zion!
For he strengthens the bars of your gates;
    he blesses your sons within you.
He makes peace in your borders;
    he fills you with the finest of the wheat.
He sends forth His command to the earth;
    his word runs swiftly.

He gives snow like wool;
   he scatters hoarfrost like ashes.
He casts forth his ice like morsels;
   who can stand before his cold?
He sends forth his word, and melts them;
   he makes his wind blow, and the waters flow.
He declares his word to Jacob,
   his statutes and ordinances to Israel.
He has not dealt thus with any other nation;
   they do not know his ordinances.
Praise the Lord!
(Psalm 147)

~~Are You Saved?~~ Are You Prepared?
Are You Preparing?

For by grace you have been saved through faith; and this is not your own doing, it is the gift of God.

Ephesians 2:8

So faith by itself, if it has no works, is dead.

James 2:17

Many Protestant Christians ask the question, "Are you saved?" Or they encourage people to "get saved." Perhaps you've been asked this question and wondered about it for yourself. I've actually been challenged with the question, "Do you know that you are going to heaven?" When I answer, "No," I'm even confronted with, "What kind of priest are you, if you don't know where you are going?"

Salvation Is a Process

The Orthodox understanding of salvation is that it doesn't happen in one finite moment. I can't point to a specific day and say, "On May 20, 2007, I was saved." I actually can't even say that "I gave my life to Christ" on a particular day. I may give my life to Christ today, but if

I sin later today, then in that moment I'm taking my life away from Christ—I'm turning my back on Him.

Rather, the journey to salvation is a process. In this process is repentance because, in our sinful nature, we continually fall away from Christ—and through repentance, we continually turn back toward Him. If I say, "I know I'm going to heaven," then I've put myself on the judgment seat in the place of God. In the same way, if we say, "There's no way that _____ is going to heaven," we've also placed ourselves on the judgment seat in place of God. The judgment is His alone. Thus, there is no way to say "I'm saved" or "I'm condemned," because the Lord will do the saving and condemning on Judgment Day. Jesus tells us so in His account of the sheep and the goats (Matt. 25:31–46): The Lord will do the separating. That's His prerogative exclusively.

The important question to ask ourselves and one another is, "Are you prepared?" or, perhaps better yet, "Are you preparing?" *Preparing* in this case refers to readying ourselves to stand before the judgment seat of Christ. In Matthew 25, Jesus will separate the sheep from the goats based on the following metrics: feeding the hungry, giving drink to the thirsty, welcoming the stranger, clothing the naked, visiting the sick, and ministering to those in prison.

Expanding on these six metrics, feeding the hungry includes not only those who are hungry for food but are hungry for attention, friendship, sympathy, mercy, understanding, and help. A stranger is not just the new person in town, but the person who is lonely, as well as the person who is a stranger to you—someone you don't know, like the people who help us in the grocery store or, for the person who works behind a counter, the customer, patient, or client. Prisons aren't just buildings with bars but circumstances that hold us captive: A learning disability, a physical handicap, poverty, and lack of dedicated parents are circumstances that trap us. How do we minister to people we meet who are sentenced to long terms in these kinds of "prisons"? How do we behave when we find ourselves "imprisoned" by some circumstance?

If we think about these things critically, we realize that we are presented with these kinds of needs every day. If you are reading this message in the morning, you will have a chance to minister to someone before the day is over. Will you recognize this opportunity and answer your call? And if you are reading this message at night, more than likely you had an opportunity today. Did you recognize it, and did you answer your call?

Some Better Questions to Ask Ourselves

In my humble opinion, the idea of "being saved" is like clinching a playoff spot on a sports team; in other words, you are guaranteed a place even if you lose every game for the rest of the season. But salvation doesn't work this way. There is no "clinching," either of salvation or condemnation. The repentant thief on the cross next to Jesus found salvation in his dying breath. And there are plenty of people who have lived "righteous" lives only to fall away from the Christian Faith later in life. It's never too late to find salvation. And we can't "claim salvation" for ourselves, because it is the Lord's to give to whomever He wishes based on His standards, not ours.

Three more appropriate questions come to mind:

+ Are you prepared for your judgment, should the Lord come for your soul tonight?
  Many of us shudder at that thought.
+ Are you *preparing* for your judgment?
  Hopefully the answer is yes for each of us. Hopefully we are living a life where we are serving according to those six metrics in Matthew 25:31–46, using the talents we've been given. (See the Parable of the Talents in Matthew 25:14–30.)

✦ Can you be prepared?

This third question is comforting because the answer is yes. We can all prepare for the judgment. We all should be preparing for it. That's why the petition for a Christian end to our lives is part of the Divine Liturgy, so that we are constantly reminded not only of where we are going but of the importance of preparing for eternity on a continual basis.

When someone asks me, "Are you saved?" I always answer, "I'm working on it, and I hope by God's grace I will be saved." I've never asked anyone if they are saved. We are continuously praying for the salvation of all.

Praise the LORD!
O give thanks to the LORD, for he is good;
    for his steadfast love endures forever!
Who can utter the mighty doings of the LORD,
    or show forth all his praise?
Blessed are they who observe justice,
    who do righteousness at all times!

Remember me, O LORD, when thou showest favor to
    thy people;
    help me when thou deliverest them;
that I may see the prosperity of thy chosen ones,
    that I may rejoice in the gladness of thy nation,
    that I may glory with Thy heritage.
(Psalm 106:1–5)

It's Never Too Late (As Long as You Are Alive)

One of the criminals who were hanged railed at him, saying, "Are you not the Christ? Save yourself and us!" But the other rebuked him, saying, "Do you not fear God, since you are under the same sentence of condemnation? And we indeed justly; for we are receiving the due reward of our deeds; but this man has done nothing wrong." And he said, "Jesus, remember me when you come into your kingdom." And he said to him, "Truly, I say to you,
today you will be with me in Paradise."

Luke 23:39–43

One of the most beautiful and hopeful things about Christianity is that it is never too late to start—provided that you are still alive. And one of the most hopeful stories in the entire Bible is the account of the repentant thief on the cross. As someone once said to me, "He was such a good thief, he stole Paradise in the last moment."

The Story of Dismas

The thief, who is not given a name in the Bible, is actually a saint in the Orthodox Church. While various Christian traditions have assigned him different names, he is known in the Orthodox world as

Dismas, which means "sunset" or "death." The apocryphal Gospel of Nicodemus refers to him.[18]

Crucifixion was the most horrific method of capital punishment that the Romans employed. It was painful, death came slowly, it was carried out in public, and it was humiliating. It was reserved for the worst of criminals. The thief was a man for whom imprisonment wasn't enough. Even execution wasn't enough. He needed crucifixion—the most heinous ending possible.

Jesus was crucified between two thieves: Dismas and another man known in tradition as Gestas, the unrepentant thief. Gestas, whose name in Greek means "to complain" or "to moan," railed at Jesus, saying, "Are you not the Christ? Save yourself and us!" (Luke 23:39). He saw Jesus as a means to cheat death and to cheat Rome. Maybe he was just in a desperate amount of pain and was shouting for any shred of relief.

The repentant thief, however, took a different approach. The sign over Jesus read "Jesus of Nazareth, the King of the Jews" (John 19:19), so the man would have had some inkling as to who Jesus was. He said, "Jesus, remember me when you come into your kingdom." And Jesus responded, "Truly, I say to you, today you will be with me in Paradise" (Luke 23:42–43).

Faith, Works, and Grace

You might be thinking, "Okay, great. Deathbed confession gets it done!" And that's true—it worked for the repentant thief. It is up to the Lord to grant Paradise to whomever He chooses. We also hold in the Orthodox Church that it is a combination of faith, works, and grace that saves us.[19]

---

18 This information is taken from orthodoxwiki.org/Dismas_the_thief.
19 The best analogy for salvation is to consider a cup, rocks, and water. The cup is a structure—our faith, the structure of what we believe. The rocks

With the thief, these three elements were actually present. He demonstrated faith as he turned to Jesus and asked Jesus to remember him. He performed only one work, and that was directed at the other thief. As the unrepentant thief railed at Jesus, the repentant one looked at him with some degree of compassion. He asked him, "Do you not fear God, since you are under the same sentence of condemnation? And we indeed justly; for we are receiving the due reward of our deeds; but this man has done nothing wrong" (Luke 23:40–41). He cared in the moment for that other man and *his* salvation. And that was enough for Jesus to pour his grace on the man, telling him that he would be the first to enter into Paradise.

Many times we are tempted to put ourselves on the judgment seat. We want to say that "for sure" someone is in heaven. As a priest, I have found that many times people want me to put some kind of stamp of approval on their loved one, proclaiming that they are in heaven, just like Protestant Christians who claim to "be saved."

But for the Orthodox, salvation is a process, not a one-time event. The best way to describe salvation is to compare it to marriage. I was married in a finite moment of time, on a specific day. I am married today, and I hope to be married a long time from now. But if I just repeated vows on my wedding day, said "I am married," and never did anything else, there is no way I'd still be married years later. Marriage isn't a one-time-for-all-time event, and neither is salvation. Both are living relationships.

---

represent works. An empty cup is not useful, and rocks spread out over a table have no order—they go everywhere. Works are supposed to be done in the context of faith; otherwise the works are ultimately self-serving. Now, put the rocks in the cup. The cup is still not full. But if we pour water into the cup of rocks, all the empty spaces are filled. Water is grace—the grace of God that completes what is lacking in every life. How big must the cup be? How many rocks must fill it? How much grace can we count on? There is no quantifying these things.

I have the potential for salvation because Jesus died for my sins. I was saved when I got baptized and took my first steps toward Him. I am being saved because of what I am doing today to follow His commandments. And ultimately I hope to be saved, but my salvation will be an act of God's grace. It is not mine to claim. I can prepare for salvation, but only the Lord can give it. How much preparation is enough? This is His decision, not mine. In the case of the thief, his short encounter with Christ was enough.

We are often tempted to put ourselves on the judgment seat to claim someone is for sure going to heaven, but many times we are also tempted to put someone in hell. We think that certain people can't possibly be going to heaven. But that destiny also is not ours to grant. Someone looking at the thief on the cross would not have slated him for Paradise, and yet the Lord did.

What we do know is that a combination of faith, works, and grace leads us into heaven. Like the thief, we know that we can find salvation even at the last moment. But the thief had an advantage: He knew he was dying. This was his last chance. For the rest of us, we usually do not know when our last moment will arrive. We should not wait to turn—or return—to Christ. As long as we are alive, it is never too late!

My soul languishes for thy salvation;
    I hope in thy word.
My eyes fail with watching for thy promise;
    I ask, "When wilt thou comfort me?"
For I have become like a wineskin in the smoke,
    yet I have not forgotten thy statutes.
How long must thy servant endure?
    When wilt thou judge those who persecute me?
Godless men have dug pitfalls for me,
      men who do not conform to thy law.

All thy commandments are sure;
    they persecute me with falsehood; help me!
They have almost made an end of me on earth;
    but I have not forsaken thy precepts.
In thy steadfast love spare my life,
    that I may keep the testimonies of thy mouth.
(Psalm 119:81–88)

It's Too Late After We Die:
The Rich Man and Lazarus

There was a rich man, who was clothed in purple and fine linen and who feasted sumptuously every day. And at his gate lay a poor man named Laz'arus, full of sores, who desired to be fed with what fell from the rich man's table; moreover the dogs came and licked his sores. The poor man died and was carried by the angels to Abraham's bosom. The rich man also died and was buried; and in Hades, being in torment, he lifted up his eyes, and saw Abraham far off and Laz'arus in his bosom. And he called out, "Father Abraham, have mercy upon me, and send Laz'arus to dip the end of his finger in water and cool my tongue; for I am in anguish in this flame." But Abraham said, "Son, remember that you in your lifetime received your good things, and Laz'arus in like manner evil things; but now he is comforted here, and you are in anguish. And besides all this, between us and you a great chasm has been fixed, in order that those who would pass from here to you may not be able, and none may cross from there to us." And he said, "Then I beg you, father, to send him to my father's house, for I have five brothers, so that he may warn them, lest they also come into this place of torment." But Abraham said, "They have Moses and the prophets; let them hear them." And he said, "No, father Abraham; but if someone goes to them from the dead, they will repent." He said to him, "If they do not hear Moses and the prophets, neither will they be convinced if someone should rise from the dead."

Luke 16:19–31

In the previous reflection about the thief on the cross, we discussed how it is never too late to come to Christ—as long as we are alive. But there is a point where repentance is not possible, and that is when we die. The Bible gives us some clues about heaven and hell, and everything I've written in this book is based on this information. Yes, there are many Church Fathers, saints, theologians, and others who have expounded on Scripture and do so in a way to help us understand it. And while is good and important to understand the things that are "around" the Bible—writings, services like the Divine Liturgy (which is based on Scripture), and traditions (also based in Scripture)—we are supposed to spend time in the Scriptures themselves so that God can reveal Himself to us in our own reading.

Let's look at this passage from Luke 16:19–31, the story of the rich man and Lazarus. Jesus presents us with two men: an unnamed rich man and Lazarus. The rich man is *very* rich. He feasts "sumptuously every day" and is "clothed in purple and fine linen." At his gate lies a poor man named Lazarus, who is covered in sores and has nothing to eat. He would be satisfied with the crumbs that fall from the rich man's table. And yet the rich man won't even give him those.

Eventually both men die, as we all will, and the angels carry Lazarus to the bosom of Abraham. We don't really get much of a visual of what this looks like, but I imagine Lazarus being embraced by Abraham and feeling safe, secure, and loved.

The rich man is in Hades, in torment. It's interesting that he is able to see Lazarus in the bosom of Abraham. Not only is he suffering in hell, he can see heaven, and he can see Lazarus there. The next clue we are given about hell is that it is hot there. The rich man is in anguish and asks Abraham to let Lazarus dip his finger in water and put it on his tongue.

Abraham then shares two things with the rich man. First, he tells him that in his lifetime he received good things, and Lazarus received evil things. The rich man was in Hades not because he was rich but because he was indifferent. He had ample opportunities to help Lazarus, and he didn't. He didn't even have to go far—the man was right at his gate. If he didn't help the man who was right at his gate, presumably he wouldn't have helped those beyond it. Second, Abraham tells him that there is a chasm between heaven and hell. Those in heaven cannot go to hell, and those in hell cannot go to heaven. Those placements are permanent.

Then the rich man implores Abraham that he has five brothers and that Abraham should send Lazarus to warn them. *Now*, all of a sudden, the rich man has a conscience; he wants to do good for someone else. He spent his whole life being self-absorbed, and now he finally wants to do the right thing. But Abraham tells him that his request won't be granted. It is too late.

Our Opportunity Is in This Life

This story is a warning for us all. If we are going to follow Christ, we have to do it in this life. You might ask, What about those who have never heard of Christ and thus never had the opportunity to come to Him? The answer there, I believe, is that those who have never heard of Christ are perhaps in a different category—perhaps He will give them a chance to believe. I don't know. It is God who sits on the judgment seat, not us. What I do know is that I'm not in that category, and neither are you.

We have had the opportunity to know Christ. And we have the opportunity to serve Christ by serving others. The rich man had ample opportunity too, at his gate, every day. And what's sad is that poor Lazarus didn't want to take the rich man's wealth; he didn't even begrudge him that. He just wanted some crumbs, and that was too much for the rich man—the crumbs he wasn't going to eat anyway. Only in death did he recognize his error and express a desire to serve others. But it was too late.

You and I must figure out how to believe and to serve today, while we are alive on earth. The ability to believe and repent ends when we die.

> For God alone my soul waits in silence;
> from him comes my salvation.
> He only is my rock and my salvation, my fortress;
> I shall not be greatly moved.

> How long will you set upon a man
> to shatter him, all of you,
> like a leaning wall, a tottering fence?
> They only plan to thrust him down from his eminence.
> They take pleasure in falsehood.
> They bless with their mouths,
> but inwardly they curse.

> For God alone my soul waits in silence,
> for my hope is from him.
> He only is my rock and my salvation,
> my fortress; I shall not be shaken.
> On God rests my deliverance and my honor;
> my mighty rock, my refuge is God.

Trust in him at all times, O people;
   pour out your heart before him;
   God is a refuge for us.
Men of low estate are but a breath,
   men of high estate are a delusion;
in the balances they go up;
   they are together lighter than a breath.
Put no confidence in extortion,
   set no vain hopes on robbery;
   if riches increase, set not your heart on them.

Once God has spoken;
   twice have I heard this:
that power belongs to God;
   and that to thee, O Lord, belongs steadfast love.
For thou dost requite a man
   according to his work.
(Psalm 62)

Tough End-of-Life Decisions

Fighting and Why It's Important

Fight the good fight of the faith; take hold of the eternal life to which you were called when you made the good confession in the presence of many witnesses.

1 Timothy 6:12

I have fought the good fight, I have finished the race, I have kept the faith.

2 Timothy 4:7

People have a hard time understanding our life on earth as it compares to eternity. To illustrate this concept, I once gave a sermon where I laid a seventy-five-foot length of rope down the middle aisle of our church. I asked everyone if they could see the rope, and they said they could. I then held up a small object in my hand and asked if anyone in the back pew could identify what I was holding. No one could. It was a paper clip. I attached it to the rope.

The lesson was simple: The rope represents eternity. The paper clip represents the span of our lives on earth, a blip compared to the span of eternity. If someone has the best life but doesn't have faith in God, backed up by works, then they should enjoy their life now because it will be followed by an eternity of misery: The paper clip of joy followed by the lengthy rope of misery. If someone has the worst life but a strong faith, they just need to persevere and hang on to their faith throughout their trials. Then they will have an eternity of happiness: The paper clip of misery followed by the lengthy rope of joy.

In the two Bible verses above, we read references to "the good fight." In an athletic contest with the goal of fighting to win, the good fight means we play by the rules and "leave everything on the field," so that even if we lose the game, it wasn't for lack of trying. We can walk away saying that we did everything we could do. A priest once said to me that he hoped to "die exhausted," having used every day and every opportunity to glorify God. To fight a good fight, to finish the race, and to keep the faith (2 Tim. 4:7) requires a solid effort all the way through the finish line of life, regardless of what life throws at us.

Medical Interventions and Care for Our Bodies

When faced with a health challenge, even one that is going to be difficult—or terminal—we are called on to "fight." But this doesn't mean that we force a ninety-five-year-old to undergo chemotherapy, or that a terminal diagnosis requires us to do everything possible to extend life. I remember when my mom was very sick years ago, her doctor used the term *recoverability* in trying to map out the best course of treatment. If a person has a treatable disease, they should seek treatment, even if it is challenging. If there is recoverability— the possibility of returning to life in some way similar to what it was before—then we should pursue that.

When someone has a serious illness, like a heart attack or a stroke, often procedures can be tried so they can recover their previous vitality, and we are called to do this. I confess that I have never been diagnosed with a serious, life-threatening illness. I've had a few close calls where doctors ordered diagnostic tests to rule out cancer, and I have acquiesced and done them, even though they are uncomfortable. This effort is part of the fighting the good fight and making sure we take advantage of the blessing of life that God has bestowed on us.

One arena in which we are expected to fight is our overall health—we are supposed to eat right, make time to exercise, and manage our stress. I'm guilty of failing in all three. Sometimes I worry that these bad habits will cause me to die prematurely. It would be a shame to stand before God at age 60 and hear Him say, "I intended for you to live to be 80, but you ate poorly, so you are here twenty years early." This reflection is as much for you, the reader, as it is for me, the writer.

God has blessed each of us with talents and with opportunities to use those talents to glorify Him and to serve others. (See Matt. 25:14–30.) Sitting on your talent or burying it in the ground is not acceptable to God. Neither is abusing our bodies and dying sooner than He intends. Neither is refusing to seek help for medical illnesses when there is recoverability.

I hope that if I am faced with a serious medical challenge, like cardiovascular disease, cancer, or a degenerative condition, I will have grace to fight a good fight and somehow keep my eyes on the prize of salvation.

We should also help and encourage others in their fight. One of my biggest fears is to have a significant setback that is treatable—cancer, for example—but requires six months or a year of medical care. In the process, I could lose my job. If people see value in one another and hold the place for someone until they can get better, that support creates motivation for fighting the good fight against disease. I know people who have lost jobs because of illness, and so not only do they lose health, they also lose purpose, vitality, identity, income, and so much more. Encouraging and helping those who are sick so that they will not suffer more losses is a gift we will all be able to give at some point.

Fighting the Good Fight

If I could choose one verse for my tombstone, it would be 2 Timothy 4:7, because not only is it the message I hope to say in defense of my life when I stand before God, it is the legacy I hope to leave behind: to be remembered for fighting a good fight, finishing the race, and keeping the faith. One challenge in fighting a good fight against illness is that it can impact our faith in a negative way. When suffering is great or goes on for a long time, people sometimes lash out at God. It is important while fighting the good fight and finishing the race that we keep the faith. It is crucial that when we see someone fighting a good fight against disease, we make sure to help safeguard their faith as well.

Our lives are like a paper clip on a rope when it comes to the span of eternity. Whatever trials we may face—medical or otherwise—we need to give it our best. And if we have fought the good fight and kept the faith, we are in good position for our "good defense before the awesome judgment seat of Christ."[20]

Forever, O Lord, thy word
 is firmly fixed in the heavens.
Thy faithfulness endures to all generations;
 thou hast established the earth, and it stands fast.
By thy appointment they stand this day;
 for all things are thy servants.
If thy law had not been my delight,
 I should have perished in my affliction.
I will never forget thy precepts;
 for by them thou has given me life.
I am thine, save me;
 for I have sought thy precepts.

---

20 *Divine Liturgy of St. John Chrysostom* (2015), 43.

The wicked lie in wait to destroy me;
    but I consider thy testimonies.
I have seen a limit to all perfection,
    but thy commandment is exceedingly broad.
(Psalm 119:89–96)

Surrender and Why It's Necessary

Then Jesus, crying with a loud voice, said, "Father, into thy hands I commit my spirit!" And having said this he breathed his last.

Luke 23:46

One of the favorite activities at summer camp is called the "trust fall." Someone stands on a platform, about five to six feet off the ground, and eight people stand underneath it. The person on the platform, with their back to the people below, falls backward and is caught by them. The first time anyone does this, it is pretty unnerving, because in order to fall, they have to surrender total control of their bodies to those catching below. There is definitely a "moment of truth" when someone is about to fall, when they wonder, "Are they *really* going to catch me?" That's normal, to have a little bit of doubt. In order to fall, though, the person has to have enough faith that those below will catch them. What helps with this is watching others do it successfully. That gives one confidence in the catchers and faith that one will be caught and not harmed.

Of course, there are some people who won't get up on the platform, or, once on the platform, they elect not to do the trust fall. There are some who try to fall but instead of falling back and allowing their weight to be equally dispersed, they go limp, sending all their weight on just two people. It's possible to actually get hurt, and to hurt others, by not doing this activity correctly.

Relinquishing Control

There are other instances in life, besides the trust fall, where we have to cede control to someone else. If you've ever been put under general anesthetic, you have to trust a doctor to render you unconscious and trust that they will bring you back. Even more common is flying on an airplane, ceding control to the pilot who will take the plane off the ground and safely bring it back down.

The ultimate trust fall is for us to close our eyes in death and fall into the unknown, trusting that God and all His angels will catch our soul, so to speak. Jesus gives the ultimate example of how to die, because at the moment of His death, He uttered the words, "Father, into thy hands I commit my spirit!" (Luke 23:46). And then, we are told in John 19:30 that "he bowed his head and gave up his spirit." Unlike Hollywood movies where a dying person struggles, stops breathing, and then their head droops, Jesus lowered His head and then gave up His spirit. He surrendered.

At the beginning of this book, we discussed why it is necessary that we die. Now, for a quick comment about why Christ had to die. There are two reasons and two comparisons with real life that will help this make sense.

First, salvation is like an algebra equation. If you take the equation $2x + 2 = 6$, $x = 2$, you arrive at the answer by subtracting two from both sides and dividing by two on both sides. Whatever happens on one side must happen on the other. When God created human beings, He made us in His *image and likeness* (Gen. 1:26) so that man could live forever, like God. We were not created to die. But after the Fall, as we have previously discussed, a Pandora's Box of consequences opened on humanity's side of the equation. God's image and likeness in us is now damaged. Now people get sick, tired, angry, frustrated, and eventually die.

This leads to the second comparison for real life: the concept of paying a remittance. Romans 6:23 says that "the wages of sin is death." In other words, because of the Fall, we now owe a debt of death. When someone has a credit card bill, or some other kind of debt, they receive a statement in the mail that comes with a "remittance," a place for payment to be made. If I owe $200 to the credit card company, I "remit" $200 in the form of a check, and the debt is paid. If I owe the money and *you* write a check to the credit card company for the $200, the credit card company won't mind. They'll clear my account to $0, regardless of who pays the debt.

And so God, through the Incarnation, sent Jesus to pay the remittance of death that we owe God because of our sins. And the way this happened was that Jesus came to earth and balanced the algebra equation, by suffering on His side, in the same way we suffer on ours, right up to the point of death. In John 19:30, before bowing His head and surrendering His spirit, Jesus uttered the words, "It is finished." In other words, the equation was now balanced. We must die. Therefore, He would die. And He died the way someone does a trust fall, He placed His total trust in God and surrendered His spirit. And the equation was now balanced.

Next on His side, He rose from the dead, ascended into heaven and sat at the right hand of the Father. The equation now again is unbalanced, because we have yet to die. If we live in faith, and die with faith, then we have the potential, through His grace, to be resurrected, ascend to heaven and sit at the right hand of God, which we know from a previous reflection will be permanent, we won't be able to fall from there if He grants us to sit at His right hand.

The previous reflection discussed how we need to put up a good fight when it comes to living, and even in dealing with illness. But at some point, we have to surrender. I've done the trust fall so many times at camp that when it comes time to do it, I actually relax, close my eyes, and just fall. Every time I'm fine—it hardly gets my heart rate up anymore. Ideally, I hope my exit from this life works in the same way. I hope that I am so comfortable with my faith and with my relationship with God that when the time comes for me to pass, I can relax, close my eyes, and just let go, confident that He is going to catch me.

In the journey of those who have serious illness and run out of treatment options, I hope the time will come when they recognize that all avenues have been pursued and now it is time to just surrender. As we will read shortly, a person's family, as well as their priest and church family, can do a lot to help someone surrender. The greatest help, though, is practicing through life: surrendering control to God in small things so that when the ultimate challenge of death comes, we are comfortable with the concept of faith—and also of surrender.

We will all be on the platform one day to make the ultimate trust fall. Seeing others do it, dying with faith, will help. Thinking about that day will also help. And building faith by trusting God throughout life will help.

O, how I love thy law!
    It is my meditation all the day.
Thy commandment makes me wiser than my enemies,
    for it is ever with me.
I have more understanding than all my teachers,
    for thy testimonies are my meditation.
I understand more than the aged,
    for I keep thy precepts.
I hold back my feet from every evil way,
    in order to keep thy word.

I do not turn aside from thy ordinances,
    for thou has taught me.
How sweet are thy words to my taste,
    sweeter than honey to my mouth!
Through thy precepts I get understanding;
    therefore I hate every false way.
(Psalm 119:97–104)

I Got My Miracle After All—John

Truly, truly, I say to you, he who hears my word and believes him who sent me, has eternal life; he does not come into judgment, but has passed from death to life.

John 5:24

One of the privileges of the priesthood is that I get to be part of the last mile of many people's lives. I do not work miracles; God does that. And I am not sharing these stories to boast about something I've accomplished. I share them with you so that you can know that death can be beautiful, not just painful—and that sometimes little miracles happen even in death.

Looking for a Miracle

On my first day as the priest of St. John in Tampa, September 1, 2004, a man came to my office door as I was unpacking boxes. He introduced himself, saying, "Hi, my name is John, and I have cancer. Some people are dying from it; I'm living with it. I am going to be a miracle."

I didn't know what to say. I think I just said, "Hi, my name is Father Stavros."

Over the course of the next few weeks, every time John wasn't having a cancer treatment, he would stop by the office and take me out to lunch. He had good tastes and introduced me to some of the finest restaurants in Tampa. We quickly became friends. I also found out that his diagnosis was pretty bleak—he had pancreatic cancer and wasn't expected to live many months. He had been diagnosed at the end of May, just over three months before I arrived.

In October, John's daughter got married. My wife and I were invited to the rehearsal dinner and were asked to sit with John. In the middle of the dinner, John whispered to me that he wasn't feeling good and that he wanted to go home. He asked if I could take him; he didn't want to ruin his daughter's day. After I dropped him at his house, I watched him struggle up the front steps. I went back to help him and asked if I could stop by his house the next morning to say a prayer for him. He said that would be nice.

The next day was Sunday, and I stopped by before church and offered a simple prayer in his kitchen: "Lord, we are not here asking for a miracle today; we'll be back to ask for that tomorrow. We just need this man to be able to walk down the aisle with his daughter and to dance with her. That is the prayer for today." God answered that prayer—John walked his daughter down the aisle and danced with her—that was a little miracle in itself.

I remember asking my spiritual father how I should pray for John. I didn't want to pray for the miracle of healing, which seemed unlikely. I also didn't want to pray for him to die, because death didn't seem imminent either. My spiritual father suggested I pray the Lord's Prayer for John—*Give us this day our daily bread* (Matt. 6:11). In other words, I should ask the Lord to give to him what he needs on a particular day. I started doing that.

Lord, You Are My Everything

November arrived. In one of our many talks I had asked John if he had ever been to confession. He hadn't. I suggested that confession was a good thing for someone in his position to do. One day he came to the church and said, "Let's do that confession thing you've been talking about."

We sat in the church for two hours. His voice was like thunder. I remember only two things that he said: One was that he had gone to the seminary but never finished and always wondered what it would be like to be a priest. The other was that he looked up at the Lord on the icon screen and said, "Lord, You are my everything. I wake up to You. I fall asleep to You. I think of You during every painful treatment. Lord, You are my everything!"

When he finished, I was speechless. His depth of spiritual maturity in those two hours was beyond description. I remember telling him that he would have been an excellent priest and that I felt like he should hear my confession. He asked if we could sing a hymn together—"O Gladsome Light," the beautiful hymn from Vespers. Most men who have contemplated the priesthood are enamored when many priests sing it. We sang it together—I sang, he harmonized. I still hear his voice when I sing it to this day. He asked me to set a goal for him—something out in the future to work toward. I asked him if we could sing a hymn together on Good Friday afternoon at the service. He agreed.

John and I continued to hang out in December and January. The treatments became more frequent and more painful, so I saw John more at the hospital than I did in restaurants. In February, John called me one day and asked me to come to the hospital. When I arrived, he said, "I'm having a small procedure tomorrow, but I know this is the end for me." John had a feeling, deep within his soul, that his life was drawing to a close. Rather than fight, he had begun to surrender, to make that last and greatest expression of faith in God, to leave his life and his soul in the hands of God.

I answered, "It's just a small procedure. I'm sure it will be fine." He insisted that it would be the end and asked if he could go for confession again. Everyone left the room, and it was just John and me. He began by saying, "This will be my last confession." It is stunning when someone says it will be the last of something. Again, I don't remember what he said.[21] At the end, he grabbed my hand and said, "Thank you for being my priest. I don't need you as a priest anymore. I just want you to walk the last mile with me as my friend." We both cried.

Four Final Requests

The next day, he had the surgery. He was right—the cancer was everywhere. There would be no more treatments. His wife asked me if I would come to the hospital and be there when they told him it was the end. I went. The doctor actually asked me if I would say the words to him, that it was the end, and then the doctor gave the reasons why. John was understandably emotional. When he collected himself, he said that he had four requests: He didn't want to die in pain, he didn't want to die in the hospital, and he wanted to stop by his church one more time, though it wouldn't be for a service. He just wanted to light a candle.

His fourth request was to ask forgiveness from someone before he died. He asked me to call a particular person and tell him that John wanted him to come by the hospital for two minutes. The man didn't need to say anything, but John wanted to ask forgiveness from him before he died. Thankfully, that happened quickly. No one knows what was said in that room besides God and those two men, but it was a magnanimous gesture on the part of each—on the part of one to come to the hospital and on the part of the other to ask

---

21　As I noted earlier, I never remember the things I hear in confession. The grace of the Holy Spirit that comes on a person to wipe away their sins comes on me also and wipes out my memories of the conversations.

forgiveness. Perhaps they forgave each other—I don't need to know. The other man died several years ago as well.

On a Thursday afternoon, February 24, an ambulance brought John to our church and rolled the stretcher in through the side door. They asked John if they should put the stretcher on the solea. He smiled and said, "No, that's where they'll put me next week. Put me in the center aisle by the pews where the people sit." John received Holy Communion. He asked if we could sing "Christ is Risen," even though it was February. He said he wouldn't make it to my first Pascha in Tampa but wanted to sing that hymn together. He apologized that he wouldn't be able to sing with me on Good Friday afternoon. We arranged for his son-in-law to sing with me then, a tradition that continues still.

Psalm 18:1–2 reads, "I love thee, O Lord, my strength. / The Lord is my rock, and my fortress, and my deliverer." Right before the Creed, the priest venerates the Holy Gifts and offers these words from Psalm 18. I took out my Liturgy books from the altar and told John, "I know that you are going to die, and I would like to have a souvenir from your life. I would like you to write your name in the margin of my Liturgy books next to this prayer, so that each time I celebrate the Divine Liturgy I will think of you and see your name written with your own hand." With a very shaky hand, John signed all my books. I still see his name today and think of him when I offer that prayer. Each time I say these words, I remember how he said, "I love You, Lord, my everything!"

Ready to Go Home

I asked John if there was anything else he needed. He motioned for me to put my ear next to his mouth. I bent down, and he whispered, "I'm ready to go home, and I'm not talking about South Tampa. I got my miracle after all."

I looked at his face. He was gazing up at the dome of the church, but it seemed like more than that. His eyes were focusing on something far away. His smile was radiant, and his face was filled with joy. I have never seen an expression like that before or since. It was as if God slid the dome off the church and showed him heaven. And for the rest of my life, I will believe that I saw a man see heaven, because he was so happy—euphoric, actually.

John passed away three days later at home, at 5:15 a.m. on Sunday, February 27, 2005. I was there. It was raining. That day was the Sunday of the Prodigal Son, the day we read about the son who returned home to his father. It was as if the city of Tampa was crying as one of her sons returned home to his Father. Of course, I was sad that I lost a friend. However, I was grateful for my friend of six months, who was like a father figure to me. That night, we had a gathering of young adults, and one of them asked me if I was nervous or sad to do John's funeral. I remember I told them I couldn't wait to do John's funeral and to tell his story.

Just before John's forty-day memorial service, his daughter called me and asked me how I would explain the concept of death to a three-year-old. I didn't have a child at the time and honestly had no idea. I told her I'd think about it and get back to her. That night I had a dream, and in my dream I was sitting on a hill, looking over the ocean. A phone was in my hand, and it rang. I answered, and on the other end I heard a familiar voice: "Hi, Father, this is John, and I want to tell you about heaven. It's wonderful here. I'm happy. We worship all the time, and I love it. Please, Father, do me this favor. Please tell my three-year-old granddaughter that Pappou helps God put the moon and the stars in the sky each night. She will understand that."

I woke up from the dream, looked at my clock, and it was 5:15 a.m.—the same hour that John had passed. I went to my computer and wrote out every detail I could remember from the dream. When

I told another priest about it and what I was going to tell John's granddaughter, he suggested I make a keepsake for her, since at three years old, she probably wouldn't remember what I would say. So I had an artist paint my dream.

When John's daughter and granddaughter came to my office to receive the gift, John's daughter asked her three-year-old to describe what she saw on the painting. John's daughter pointed out a small hand in the corner holding the moon and the stars. When asked whose hand this was, the little girl answered, "That's Pappou's hand."

There is one more piece to this story, a gift that keeps on giving. I have a very strong sense of John's presence two times a year. One is on the Sunday of the Prodigal Son, right before Lent. The other is when we sing the hymn "O Gladsome Light" on Good Friday afternoon at Vespers. In both instances, I feel a presence next to me for a few moments, and I know that it is John.

Memory eternal, John!

I will love thee, O LORD, my strength.
The LORD is my rock, and my fortress and my deliverer,
    my God, my rock, in whom I take refuge,
    my shield, and the horn of my salvation, my stronghold.
I call upon the LORD, who is worthy to be praised.

This God—his way is perfect;
    the promise of the LORD proves true;
    he is a shield for all those who take refuge in him.

For who is God, but the LORD?
    And who is a rock, except our God?
The God who girded me with strength,
    and made my way safe.

The LORD lives; and blessed be my rock,
    and exalted be the God of my salvation.

For this I will extol thee, O LORD, among the nations,
    and sing praises to thy name.
(Psalm 18:1–3, 30–32, 46, 49)

It Is Not Our Right to Play God,
Either to Keep Life Going or to End It

Our Father who art in heaven,
Hallowed be thy name.
Thy kingdom come,
Thy will be done,
On earth as it is in heaven.

Matthew 6:9–10

This reflection focuses on the decision to fight for life or to stop treatment. It is one of the trickier ones to write because there isn't an exact, correct answer for every person and every situation. We've already discussed why it is important to fight for life and also why it is necessary to surrender. The challenge for us all is knowing how long to fight and when to surrender. The other challenge is the temptation to put our will in front of God's will regarding the end of life. Do we allow the talents of doctors, who have been called by God to be His vessels, to fight to extend life? On the other hand, if all signs point to God calling someone "home," at what point do we discontinue treatment? There are no easy answers.

Refusing to Let Go

Very early in my priesthood, I was visiting a parishioner in the hospital, and a nurse came bursting into the room. She told me they needed a priest in the next room "for the last rites" because someone was "coding."

After telling her I was not Catholic and that the Orthodox Church doesn't have last rites,[22] she said there was no time and that I should come and do something. Upon entering the room, I saw an elderly man, whom I later found out was 84. The medical team was using a defibrillator to try to revive him after his heart stopped beating. I'm not a doctor, but my understanding of a defibrillator is that it can be used every couple of minutes for a period of time. After then, if it has failed to restart the heart, the patient is declared dead.

The elderly man's son was also in the room. Every two minutes or so, the medical personnel asked him if they should administer another shock—if he wanted them to keep trying. He responded with a "yes" each time. Each shock caused the man to elevate off the bed. The sheets had fallen off him, and several tubes were attached to various parts of his body. Each shock looked very painful.

After the third shock I remember thinking, *Just let him go!* But the man insisted they keep trying. After five or six shocks, they told him that the window for reviving his father had closed and that he had passed away. The son nodded his head. Each medical person then removed a tube from the man's body, and they left the room.[23]

As the son was literally saying, "Hit him again," I remember thinking, *Are you out of your mind, letting them do this repeatedly to your father?* And when it was finally over, I thought, *Are you happy now?* and *There has to be a better way than this.*

---

22   See page 169, "We Don't Have Last Rites, but We Have a Prayer."
23   This was in 1999, so some medical practices no doubt have changed since then.

Making End-of-Life Wishes Known

As I have already mentioned, I am a big proponent of parents telling their children their wishes, specifically regarding do-not-resuscitate (DNR) orders and making very clear which measures they are comfortable with and which ones they are not. I have watched people in their 80s with a feeding tube, a tracheostomy tube for breathing, a catheter to void the bladder, and dialysis to clean toxins from the blood. In these cases, literally everything is being done to support life artificially.

I don't think I would want any of these things—not in my 80s. If I was in a car wreck in my 50s and some of these things were needed as temporary measures to let an otherwise healthy body recover, that would be fine. But if they are needed to keep an otherwise unhealthy body going, I would not want that. Realize that I said "*I* would not want that"—there are other people who would. It is important for us to ask our parents what they want, and it is important for parents to tell their family what they want. And for those of us who are getting older and have children, it is important to tell them what we want.

Discussing Recoverability

One word I have learned from my mom's experience of death and from my years of ministering to people with very serious medical conditions is *recoverability*. People who have been in a car accident, or who have had a serious heart attack or stroke, may not recover and be the same people they were before. How much will they recover? The answer to this question plays a role, I believe, in how much critical support they are given. Again, speaking for myself only, if I had a serious accident or medical episode and had only a small chance to recover, I would hope to be "let go."

On the other hand, if there was a great chance to recover, I would want to try any means possible. The question then becomes, What should we do if a patient can only recover 40 percent, or 20 percent? What do we do then? I'm not giving an answer here—these are things to be discussed with doctors and with family members. But they should be discussed, and in most cases, people do not want to have these conversations.

It is often a very difficult decision to stop life support, because a family member might think they are killing someone, even if they have no chance for recoverability. It is important to talk specifically about this, because if there is no clear decision, medical personnel will do everything, including life support, unless they are told not to. In my experience, there is one specific time when support should be discontinued: when brain functioning has ceased—in other words, when someone has been declared "brain dead." A scan can tell how much, if any, brain functioning there is.

In the Orthodox Church, we believe that the human body is composed of body, mind, and spirit (soul). The spirit is tied to the mind because we are "rational" people. We believe that the soul is present in the body from the moment of conception until the time when the soul departs the body, which coincides with the death of the mind. Sometimes body and mind stop working at the same time. Sometimes the mind stops working, but life support keeps the body breathing artificially. We believe that the soul leaves with the mind, since once the mind has gone, there is no ability to believe, comprehend, repent, or do any of the things we do as Christians.

It is possible for a person to be "brain dead," but the chest still rises and falls with life support. People then think the person is still "alive" because they look alive. But once brain function ceases, it does not come back. At that point, the preferable course of action is to remove support and let the body stop. This usually happens quickly because the brain has stopped working, and with it, the rest of the body functions cease. Again, the challenge is knowing what to do if there is limited brain function. This is where the discussion on recoverability needs to happen with doctors, and the family needs to have discernment through prayer.

Finally, the family needs to understand that life will end for everyone at some point. There oftentimes comes a critical moment relating to the end of life when it's time to fight, as well as a moment when it is time to stop. Many times it is hard to know what to do.

It is important to talk about and write down wishes for end of life and the level of care that we want. It is important to understand recoverability. And it is important to discern where the line is for "fighting" for life to continue and when it is time to let a person go to God.

Thy word is a lamp to my feet
    and a light to my path.
I have sworn an oath and confirmed it,
    to observe thy righteous ordinances.
I am sorely afflicted;
    give me life, O Lord, according to thy word!
Accept my offerings of praise, O Lord,
    and teach me thy ordinances.
I hold my life in my hand continually,
    but I do not forget thy law.
The wicked have laid a snare for me,
    but I do not stray from thy precepts.
Thy testimonies are my heritage for ever;
    yea, they are the joy of my heart.
I incline my heart to perform thy statutes
    for ever, to the end.
(Psalm 119:105–112)

Hospice Fulfills the Liturgy's Petition for the End of Life

Even though I walk through the valley of the shadow of death,
I fear no evil;
for thou art with me;
thy rod and thy staff,
they comfort me.

Psalm 23:4

Two of the things people worry about when it comes to the end of life are dying in a hospital and being in pain. Hospice care is a special ministry that helps reduce these two worries. People become eligible for hospice if a doctor declares that a person has less than six months to live, and if a patient no longer wishes to fight illness but to be kept comfortable. There are, of course, many instances where someone in hospice care lives longer than six months, and there are even occasions when someone resumes treatment and leaves hospice care. Utilizing hospice may mean that death is imminent, but that is not always the case.

Benefits of Hospice Care

Both my parents died at home while under hospice care. (My mom passed in my brother's home.) Both had pain management that made their final hours more comfortable. There are people who question the ethics of hospice care, as well as the use of morphine. Having utilized this ministry for both my parents, and having seen it used with countless other people I have ministered to at the end of life, I find hospice to be an answer to our liturgical prayer for a painless, blameless, and peaceful end. In fact, in looking at the three aspects of this prayer, confession helps with the "blameless" aspect, family gives the "peaceful" component, and hospice takes care of the "painless" part.

I've seen people live for many months under hospice care, and I've seen family call for hospice in the final days, either to help the patient get back home or to pass away comfortably in a hospice facility. Hospice provides hospital beds and other things you'd find in a medical facility, right in a person's home. Hospice facilities are also available when it is not possible for someone to come home. These places remind me of hotels—they have private rooms and adequate space for family to gather around, and they usually provide a place for some family members to stay overnight as well as nice grounds for both patient and caregiver to get out into the fresh air. Hospice also provides a team of people, like chaplains and social workers, who help with advance directives and counseling. And after death has occurred, hospice offers programs to help people grieve. My experience with hospice has generally been positive.

The Role of Medical Personnel in the Dying Process

As we look at case studies of people who have passed away and reflect on the role of family members and faith in the dying process, I also want to spend some time considering others who have an important role at the end of life: medical personnel. Some of them work for hospice, where every patient dies. There are no happy endings where people recover—every case ends in death and in collateral sadness for those left behind, including the hospice workers.

Then there are the medical people who work hard to save lives but who often are not able to do so. I have a friend who is a nurse in the cardiac ICU. Many of her patients die. For someone whose life work is to help people recover, this could get demoralizing if approached in the wrong way. I have told my friend, and many other medical professionals, that the role of the doctor and nurse is to provide an opportunity for healing.

There is a really important distinction between healing and *providing an opportunity* for healing. Healing can only occur with cooperation between medical professional and patient, and the illness must also be treatable. This is true throughout life, even in situations where death is not a threat. Take, for instance, the patient who has a broken arm. A doctor can set the arm in a cast, but the patient has to keep the cast on. I remember a friend in elementary school who broke his arm. The cast was set during a hot summer. My friend used to scratch his arm by putting a hanger between the cast and his skin. The cast became so loose that my friend could take it on and off, which he did. (Of course, I was about eight years old at the time and didn't have the thought that this might be a bad idea.)

When it was time to take the cast off, the doctor brought out the saw to cut it. My friend said, "You don't need that," took off the cast, and handed it to the doctor. A quick X-ray revealed the arm was still broken, and my friend spent another six weeks in a cast. When there is hope for healing, as with a broken arm, the medical professional provides the path, and the patient needs to follow that path.

When there is no hope for healing, as is the case with hospice, or there is a strong possibility that there will be no healing, such as in the ICU, then the medical professional takes on the role of "emcee" of the dying process. They help facilitate the painless end that we pray for. And certainly, there is dignity in that. I have told my friend, the ICU nurse, that for her patients who are not going to get better, she provides encouragement and explanation as well as comfort and pain management. Her work helps the patient's family feel encouraged, understand what is going on, and experience comfort in their emotional pain. I have a great respect for people who work with patients who are at the end of life and who can appreciate their role for what it is—an actual answer to our prayer for a painless ending.

Hospice as a Setting for the Ultimate Triumph

Rather than look at hospice as a white flag of surrender, I think it is better to look at it as a place of triumph. The greatest miracle is not healing, but God opening the doors of heaven to let another person enter. Some medical personnel are charged with the opportunity to provide healing and to work in concert with God—knowingly or unknowingly—to facilitate the miracle of improved health. And some medical personnel work in places where healing rarely occurs. Their role is to ensure that the patient is ready to die—emotionally and especially spiritually. Certainly, a priest can and should be present to help someone pass away without blame and with an opportunity to talk about their faith. But the priest can't be around twenty-four hours a day like medical personnel can be. And the intimate bond between patient and caregiver often helps facilitate that painless end in a better way than any priest could.

It takes a lot of courage to put your loved one under hospice care. And it takes a lot of courage to work in this field, knowing that virtually every patient dies. While medical personnel may not be able to provide the miracle of healing for every patient, they can help facilitate the miracle of exiting this life in a faithful way. And with this point of view, both hospice personnel and hospital staff have the potential for experiencing a miracle every time, with every patient, no matter how sick they are—either the miracle of extending life or the miracle of helping someone enter into eternal life.

I have a lot of respect for doctors and nurses who minister to the dying. Please keep hospice in mind for that last journey. The staff plays a significant role in helping to provide the "painless, blameless, peaceful" end for which we pray.

To Thee, O Lord, I lift up my soul.
O my God, in thee I trust,
    let me not be put to shame;
    let not my enemies exult over me.
Yea, let none that wait for thee be put to shame;
    let them be ashamed who are wantonly treacherous.

Make me to know thy ways, O Lord;
    teach me thy paths.
Lead me in thy truth, and teach me;
    for thou art the God of my salvation;
    for thee I wait all the day long.

Be mindful of thy mercy, O Lord, and of thy steadfast love,
    for they have been from of old.
Remember not the sins of my youth, or my transgressions;
    according to thy steadfast love remember me,
    for thy goodness' sake, O Lord!
Good and upright is the Lord;
    therefore he instructs sinners in the way.
He leads the humble in what is right,
    and teaches the humble his way.
All the paths of the Lord are steadfast love and faithfulness,
    for those who keep his covenant and his testimonies.

For thy name's sake, O LORD,
  pardon my guilt, for it is great.
Who is the man that fears the LORD?
  Him will he instruct in the way that he should choose.
He himself shall abide in prosperity
  and his children shall possess the land.
The friendship of the LORD is for those who fear him,
  and he makes known to them his covenant.
My eyes are ever toward the LORD,
  for he will pluck my feet out of the net.

Turn thou to me, and be gracious to me;
  for I am lonely and afflicted.
Relieve the troubles of my heart,
  and bring me out of my distresses.
Consider my affliction and my trouble,
  and forgive all my sins.

Consider how many are my foes,
  and with what violent hatred they hate me.
Oh guard my life, and deliver me;
  let me not be put to shame, for I take refuge in thee.
May integrity and uprightness preserve me,
  for I wait for thee.
Redeem Israel, O God,
  out of all his troubles.
(Psalm 25)

The Role of Family in Death

Doing the Best That You Can

And he also who had the two talents came forward, saying, "Master, you delivered to me two talents; here I have made two talents more." His master said to him, "Well done, good and faithful servant; you have been faithful over a little, I will set you over much; enter into the joy of your master."

Matthew 25:22–23

I have referred to the Parable of the Talents (Matt. 25:14–30) several times in this book already. There are so many lessons to be taken from it and applied to life's situations, including the end of life. These verses above refer to the man who was entrusted two talents. As you may recall, another was entrusted five, and he made five more and ended up with ten. The one with two made two more and ended up with four. When the master called the servants to give account for what they had done with what they had been given, he was equally pleased with the man who ended up with four as he was with the man who ended up with ten. The reason? They did the best they could with what they had been given. Everyone has different opportunities, and it's what we make of those opportunities that matters. I will always believe that God rewards effort more than outcome. This parable confirms that.

This section of the book will focus on the role of family in the dying process. Every family and every circumstance regarding the end of life is different, and each brings its own set of challenges. In some situations, the dying person is surrounded by a big family who lives nearby and can help out with medical needs, or they are able to rotate relatives taking care of them so that they can stay home. They also can rotate visiting relatives to make sure there is always someone at the hospital bedside. This is obviously the ideal. As the saying goes, "Many hands make light work." A large family who live near one another makes for a less challenging—albeit still difficult—time in looking after a loved one who is sick.

Sometimes family members volunteer to take in a loved one to live with them. That is certainly admirable, though it does put some stress and strain on the host family. The rhythm of life in their household is now altered, or sometimes completely disrupted.

But some people have small families—for instance, one child or only one child who lives near them. A lot of responsibility falls on that child, which also can be difficult. In other situations, no one lives near the family member who is ill, and children have to make a decision to move a parent closer to them or into some kind of assisted living facility.

The Struggle and Guilt of Too Many Responsibilities

There are instances when keeping someone at home becomes impossible because of the level of care needed, the physical size of the patient, or the lack of helpers. That's a tough decision. People try to balance raising children, holding down jobs, and maintaining a home while also trying to have a social life, a good marriage, time for rest, and involvement in church community. All these commitments are hard to juggle under normal circumstances, and providing care for a loved one adds more to the mix. It gets complicated. Mixed with the stress and fatigue of all of these responsibilities is the guilt of not being able to do more. And, let's be honest—some parents or grandparents are not the best patients or the most appreciative. They can make their children or grandchildren feel guilty on top of the sadness with which they are already wrestling.

Both my parents passed in California, where they lived. I lived in Florida during the last years of their lives, and my ability to visit them was limited. I wasn't in California when either of them passed away, though thankfully I was able to get home to say a meaningful good-bye to each. My father died at his home with my mother able to take care of him. My mother passed at my brother's home, and a lot of burden fell on him. He did an amazing job with both our parents, balancing the demands of his life with taking care of them. Do I have some guilt? A little. Could I have done better? Perhaps. I tried to stay involved in their care as best I could. When I went to California to visit them, I spent all my time with them. I didn't go out with friends or do other things besides hang out with them.

My in-laws live in Hawaii. They are too old to travel, and this means vacation time and travel money go to getting there. Sometimes it means that my wife and son spend Christmas there while I stay in Florida without them, since I have to work on Christmas. This arrangement works for us.

Giving What You Can

Whatever your circumstances, I want to encourage you to do the best you can in taking care of aging parents. If you've given your best, there is nothing else left to give. We are not all blessed to have parents who live near us. Circumstances beyond our control may dictate what we can do. In the Parable of the Talents quoted at the beginning this chapter (Matt. 25:14–30), three servants were each entrusted with a different number of talents, each was dealt a different hand.

The master rewarded the one who ended up with four talents in the same way that he rewarded the one who ended up with ten, since they each made the most of what they had been entrusted. In the case of taking care of our parents, not everyone will be dealt the same set of circumstances. We simply need to do the best we can with the circumstances we have been dealt.

On the flip side, the parents who are aging need to show consideration for their children and grandchildren—to be grateful for care rather than demanding of it; to be appreciative and not lay guilt trips on children. As parents get older, they need to think about downsizing or at least getting rid of things so that their children aren't burdened with extensive cleanups of their homes.

I once saw a graphic of a garage so full of stuff the door could barely shut, with a parent saying to their child, "One day you will inherit all of this." The parent said it with pride, as in, "Look at all the stuff I'm leaving you!" But the child thought, *Look at the mess you are leaving me.* I have gone through my parents' house and taken what I want. Surprisingly, it was not much. I have plenty of stuff, and I don't need their furniture or knick-knacks.

Family plays a critical role in our lives, giving us meaning, depth, and joy. The role of family is especially important at the end. Just as there is no "best time" to have a child, likewise there is no good time for someone to pass away. People get sick and come to the end of life, and the caregiving children adjust. For those who are taking care of aging parents, and for aging parents whose children are taking care of them, patience, empathy, compassion, and gratitude go a long way. If people focus on doing their best, whether offering care or receiving it, this will go a long way to ensuring that the final chapter of someone's life is lived with love and kindness. This will set the stage for a Christian and peaceful end to life.

One motto I have used in my life is, "The best I can with what I have on a given day." We all have different circumstances. The challenge is to do the best we can in them, and when we've done so, to be okay with that!

> I hate double-minded men,
>> but I love thy law.
> Thou art my hiding place and my shield;
>> I hope in thy word.
> Depart from me, you evildoers,
>> that I may keep the commandments of my God.
> Uphold me according to thy promise, that I may live,
>> and let me not be put to shame in my hope!
> Hold me up, that I may be safe
>> and have regard for thy statutes continually!
> Thou dost spurn all who go astray from thy statutes;
>> yea, their cunning is in vain.
> All the wicked of the earth thou dost count as dross;
>> therefore, I love thy testimonies.
> My flesh trembles for fear of thee,
>> and I am afraid of thy judgments.
> (Psalm 119:113–120)

Watch Your Language and Hold Hands—Helpful Hints

But Moses' hands grew weary; so they took a stone and put it under him, and he sat upon it, and Aaron and Hur held up his hands, one on one side, and the other on the other side; so his hands were steady until the going down of the sun.

Exodus 17:12

Years ago, I was called to the hospital to visit a man named Yianni, who was in a coma. Everyone, including the hospital personnel, thought that he was about to die. His sister was sobbing, and in between sobs, she wanted to discuss his funeral arrangements.

I had heard of the idea that a person's hearing is the last thing to go,[24] and I suggested to her that perhaps we should take this conversation outside of the room. Yianni might not like to hear us talking about his funeral when he was still fighting to live.

A few days later, I went to the hospital to see Yianni and was shocked when I went into his room and found him sitting up in bed eating. "Yianni," I exclaimed, now shedding a tear of my own, "I never thought I would talk to you again."

24　Bryan Robinson, PhD, "What Happens As We're Dying? The First And Last Things To Go," forbes.com.

Yianni answered, "Yes, they say I'll live a little longer, I guess. But hey, thanks for taking my sister out of the room to talk about my funeral plans. I was actually getting annoyed about that."

What to Say and Do—and Words to Avoid

There are definitely some things that are helpful in hospital and end-of-life settings and certain things that aren't. Here are some suggestions.

1. **Watch what you say.** People can hear even if they are not conscious or don't seem to be aware. Don't discuss funeral plans, and certainly don't argue about disconnecting life support in their presence.

2. **Touch your loved one.** People can tell the difference between a "clinical" touch and a personal touch. There are lots of touches in the hospital—medical staff are constantly checking vital signs, drawing blood, checking on an IV, and other things. Patients can feel the intent of a nurse touching their arm to check vitals versus a family member offering a loving touch.

3. **Sing or play music.** Music evokes emotion. This is why at a birthday party we sing "Happy Birthday" rather than just say the words. Some songs make us smile, and sometimes songs even make us cry. For people with a mental impairment because of a stroke or dementia, sometimes songs take them back to younger, healthier, and happier times. I've seen people perk up and actually sing along to a song then go back into their world of silence.

   If a loved one had been in the choir or loved worship, play the Divine Liturgy on a speaker. In today's age of livestreamed services on Sundays or feast days, show them a video of the Liturgy from their home parish so they can hear and see something familiar. Read the Bible aloud, starting with the four Gospels. It's not too late to hear Jesus' message, hear the comforting words of psalms, or hear about the resurrection from the dead.

4. **Don't patronize.** There are two things I hear a lot in hospitals that I would not want to hear if I were a patient. First, do not compliment people for basic things. Many times family members make comments like, "He was able to eat all by himself" or "Great job going to the bathroom!" But most patients have accomplished lots of things in their lives—they've owned businesses, raised children, managed coworkers, run a classroom. Complimenting someone for something so basic can be demeaning.

The second thing well-meaning people often say is, "Just get home, and we will do everything for you." This, in my opinion, is like saying, "We want to keep you around like an heirloom that we will take off the shelf and dust occasionally." It would be better to encourage a loved one by saying, "I hope you get better because I'm counting on you to (fill in the blank)."

Make Memories While You Can

Reminiscing about old times and hearing stories from the patient's childhood is fun and provides insight that will be impossible to get after they die. Make videos, take notes, ask questions. If the person who is dying has the ability to do so, they can write letters, make videos, and leave voicemails. I still have a voice message from my mom, and a few other people who have passed, that I listen to periodically. I have my dad's voice on a video.

There is value in a person's handwriting, knowing that they placed their hand on something. My dad used to weigh himself every day for years, and he would write down the number on a scrap of paper. When I was home after he passed, my mom asked me if there was anything I wanted to take back with me. I went through his dresser and found the papers with his weight written on them, including his last entry two days before he died. I decided to keep that paper, which was the last thing Dad wrote. Even though it is just a bunch of numbers and dates, it means something to me.

We should all write notes to our children for events in the future—for example, one for when they graduate high school, one perhaps for when they graduate college, and one for the day of their wedding—just in case we are not alive for those occasions. What a nice gift to receive a handwritten note or video from a grandparent or parent on a special day when they are not alive to attend.

When Your Loved One Slips Away Privately

Finally, when it comes to the very end of life—the last moments— I'm convinced that the dying are able to choose the people they want to be present in the room. There have been many instances when family is around constantly, then at the moment they step outside because nurses are doing something, death comes. It is almost as if the dying person is sparing their family from witnessing the final moment. Many people pass away in the middle of the night, I think, just for this reason.

Once I did an exercise of answering the question, "What would you do if you had twenty-four hours to live?" (This assumes I am lucid and still able to do things.) I wrote that in my last twenty-four hours, I would want to go to confession, receive Holy Communion, eat a favorite food like ice cream, and see close friends and family. In my final hours, I would want to see my wife and son together then spend time with each alone. And in my very last hour, I would actually want to spend that time alone, in prayer and in thought, preparing to meet the Lord. That's not because I don't love my family. However, at the *very* end, I would want *all* my thoughts on the Lord, my personal repentance, salvation, and everlasting life. Thus, for those of us who are left behind, we should not feel guilty if we are at the bedside constantly, then our loved passes when we've stepped away for five minutes.

The words from Exodus 17:12 that open this chapter refer to a battle of the Israelites with the Amalekites. Every time Moses held up his hands, Israel prevailed, and when he lowered his hands, Amalek prevailed. Moses needed help holding up his hands, but perhaps, at times, his adrenaline kicked in and he could hold them up himself. This is a good lesson for all of us. We should be sensitive to helping our loved ones appropriately. There will be times when holding their hands and other measures are appropriate and helpful; at other times they might just wish to be alone with their thoughts.

Be thoughtful, sensitive, and present for your loved ones, especially when their passing is imminent.

Blessed is he whose transgression is forgiven,
    whose sin is covered.
Blessed is the man to whom the Lord imputes no iniquity,
    and in whose spirit there is no deceit.

When I declared not my sin, my body wasted away
    through my groaning all day long.
For day and night thy hand was heavy upon me;
    my strength was dried up as by the heat of summer.

I acknowledged my sin to thee,
    and I did not hide my iniquity;
I said, "I will confess my transgressions to the Lord";
    then thou didst forgive the guilt of my sin.

Therefore let everyone who is godly
    offer prayer to thee;
at a time of distress, in the rush of great waters,
    they shall not reach him.
Thou art a hiding place for me,
    thou preservest me from trouble;
    thou dost encompass me with deliverance.
I will instruct you and teach you
    the way you should go;
    I will counsel you with my eye upon you.
Be not like a horse or a mule, without understanding,
    which must be curbed with bit and bridle,
    else it will not keep with you.

Many are the pangs of the wicked;
    but steadfast love surrounds him who trusts in the LORD.
Be glad in the LORD, and rejoice, O righteous,
    and shout for joy, all you upright in the LORD!
(Psalm 32)

The Gift of Freedom—Mom

For you were called to freedom, brethren; only do not use your freedom as an opportunity for the flesh, but through love be servants of one another.

Galatians 5:13

We've all seen movies that involve scenes from prison. Chains, bars, being controlled by others, and fear mark the loss of freedom. When someone is released from prison after many years—think of the character "Brooks" in *Shawshank Redemption*—the world has passed them by, and they can't reintegrate back into society.

The Power of Choice for Those Who Are Ill

Just the thought of prison is enough to steer many away from the idea of breaking the law. And yet, when someone is seriously ill or dying, the loss of freedom associated with illness makes the person feel like they are in prison. All of a sudden they are "restrained" by being connected to an IV pole. Familiar clothes are replaced with a hospital gown. People who have an impressive resume of accomplishments are now told what to do and when to do it, and they are subject to an array of painful treatments and unpleasant touches. Any objection might get them labeled a "problem patient."

Frightened family members insist everything be done, without necessarily consulting their loved one who is in the hospital bed. Medical staff come in to do things and sometimes aren't clear why they are doing it, and in many instances the family tells the patient to go along with everything. Away from the hospital, as a patient battles disease, they might lose their job, which will only wait so long for a worker to return. If that job is something specialized, like being a priest, the result is either a permanent loss of income or a need to uproot and move in order to work again. And on top of all this, the patient is often in pain, nauseous, confused, and doesn't have all their faculties.

This paints a grim picture, and that is intentional. One of the things we prize most in our life is freedom—freedom to get up, get dressed, get in our car and drive somewhere, eat what we want, go to a job and make money, to be in control of our lives. The loss of freedom, for me and for many people, is terrifying. Losing a job and the ability to make an income, losing hope in getting better—I've had nightmares about all of these.

Three Kinds of Patients

There are three kinds of patients—those who will make a full recovery after a period of time, those who will recover but not fully, and those who have a terminal illness. Each will experience a loss of freedom, but in a different way.

Let's examine the person who is going to get better after a period of time. Let's say someone has cancer and will undergo a few cycles of chemotherapy. This is going to wreak havoc on their ability to do everyday activities, but they will return to normalcy eventually. This person will probably fear losing their job, income, and home, in addition to their fears of discomfort in recovery. As I said, I fear this. People will only be understanding with a sick person for so long before thinking about finding a replacement. And such a temporary situation, be it cancer or a car wreck, could happen to anyone at any age.

A willingness to wait and allow someone to recover from illness will help the patient cope with treatment and recovery and will give them something for which to strive. Taking away someone's employment, for example, will make it harder to stay motivated to get better; it will leave a patient wondering, *What am I striving to get better for?* We need to remember that there is a mental component to most physical ailments. As a person battles with physical illness, they are at a higher risk for anxiety and depression. The people around the patient can help fight this by offering reassurance that they will understand and be willing to restore what was lost once the long process of healing is complete.

Now consider the patient who will not fully recover. They will have to cope with the loss of life as they knew it and adjust to a new normal, with a lesser level of freedom than they enjoyed before. This new normal will definitely put someone at risk for a mental crash. Giving them as much freedom and as many choices as possible will be helpful.

Then there is the patient who isn't going to recover, who has a terminal illness. Allowing this person to help direct their care, make their own choices, and not be manipulated by the others around them shows both love and kindness. These choices, though limited, preserve their freedom and dignity and probably will go a long way in preserving their mental state and their spiritual one as well.

Putting the Ball in Mom's Court

In 2008, my mom was diagnosed with non-Hodgkins lymphoma. Within a few days her life went from normal to almost over. She began an aggressive cycle of chemotherapy that triggered a cardiac event. I flew back to California from Florida on very short notice, and when I greeted my mom, she was not only near death, she was very agitated about the treatments that were being proposed for her.

It turns out that the medical personnel were doing things without telling her what they were doing or why they were doing it. Or maybe she was having a hard time understanding it. In their defense, time was of the essence, as my mom was near death. However, even though she was very physically ill, she still had all her mental capacities. I remember asking the staff if I could speak to my mom in private, with no one else in the room. They said I could have a maximum of twenty minutes alone before the next intervention would have to take place. I remember talking to my mom and her complaining that they were just "doing things" to her without her permission.

I told her that her condition would be fatal without some quick and radical treatment. She was facing a steep climb up a tall mountain, and if she didn't start climbing, she would die within a short amount of time. I also told her that if she started "climbing" and decided at some point she wanted to stop, we would support her decision. But if she could make the steep climb, there was a chance she might even recover and beat cancer.

Once we put the ball in her court, Mom agreed to the aggressive—and painful—treatment, because she finally felt that she was deciding and that we weren't making decisions for her. My mom beat non-Hodgkins lymphoma in six months. It recurred three more times, she beat it twice, and she died from it in August 2021. Without giving her the gift of freedom, she probably would have passed away in September 2008.

The Gift of Freedom

Allowing a person freedom even in extreme illness is a gift—a gift that preserves both dignity and the person's mental state. It helps them keep a measure of control in the midst of losing so much control due to illness. If I ever get really sick and find myself with limited options, I hope that those around me will allow me freedom over the choices I will have. And if there is a chance to recover, I hope they will give me freedom to work toward resuming some sense of normalcy, holding open the roles that I treasure in the patient hope that I will return to them. In turn, I hope that if I encounter people in this position, I will always give them the same freedoms I hope to receive.

The word *empathy* literally means "in the suffering." To sympathize is to feel bad for someone. To empathize is to feel bad *with* someone—to put yourself in their shoes. To be able to see ourselves in a person who is suffering or dying—to empathize with them—will motivate us to help preserve their freedom to the greatest extent possible. Freedom is one of the greatest gifts we can give to one who is suffering.

Memory eternal, Mom!

Out of my distress I called on the LORD;
    the LORD answered me and set me free.
With the LORD on my side I do not fear.
    What can man do to me?
The LORD is on my side to help me;
    I shall look in triumph on those who hate me.
It is better to take refuge in the LORD
    than to put confidence in man.
It is better to take refuge in the LORD
    than to put confidence in princes.

All nations surrounded me;
    in the name of the LORD I cut them off!
They surrounded me, surrounded me on every side;

in the name of the LORD I cut them off!
They surrounded me like bees,
    they blazed like a fire of thorns;
    in the name of the LORD I cut them off!
I was pushed hard, so that I was falling,
    but the LORD helped me.
The LORD is my strength and my song;
    he has become my salvation.
(Psalm 118:5–14)

The Final Struggle

I wait for the LORD, my soul waits,
and in his word I hope;
my soul waits for the LORD.

Psalm 130:5–6

One of the hymns from the funeral service reads, "Alas! What a struggle it is for the soul to separate from the body."[25] I would imagine that the soul's final struggle is a conflict between a longing for God and a love of family. Imagine the two eyes of our bodies—one looks at God and sees His majesty as He beckons us to return to Him. The other sees the family, the friends, the life we've known, the joys we've had. And now there is a conflict. The conflict eventually ends because a person's body shuts down. However, this conflict, I believe, can be resolved more quickly if the family gives the dying person permission to put both eyes on God and go to Him. In a sense you might say that the family breaks the tie.

In the previous reflection we talked about the gift of freedom. The ultimate gift of freedom to give to a loved one is the freedom to go to God.

---

25 Rev. Spencer T. Kezios, *Servants and Sacraments, Book Three* (Narthex Press, 1995), 17.

Releasing Our Loved Ones to God

And it happens just by saying it. Many times, families are begging and pleading for someone to hold on and there literally is a struggle for life to end—almost like an internal conflict going on inside the person who is dying, who doesn't want to disappoint loved ones by "giving up." But at other times, family members go one by one and express that it's okay for their loved one to go to God. This then happens quickly and peacefully. I have seen other examples where almost everyone in the family is ready to let go except one person who is holding out, pleading for their loved one to keep fighting. Then within the family there are fights for this person to let go. I've seen all of these things in ministry, and they can leave a lot of residual pain and guilt after the eventual death occurs.

When I was a kid, many of my peers enjoyed jumping rope. I wasn't one of them. I was never really very coordinated with that. When two people are holding one rope, the person jumping can just start jumping when the swinging of the one rope begins. When there are two ropes involved, double-jumping, the two people who are swinging two ropes each begin swinging the ropes in opposite directions. The person who is about to jump stands outside the ropes and, using their arms, they begin to time the ropes. When the timing is in sync for everyone, they hop in the middle and begin jumping.

In a similar way, it is important that a family helps someone who is dying to "get their timing down" so that they are in the proper spiritual and emotional rhythm to pass away from this life in a painless, blameless, and peaceful way. Part of that timing is spiritual—receiving Holy Communion, confession, and prayer from a priest. Part of that timing is physical; this is the pain management and medical care offered by the professionals. And part of that timing is emotional. This emotional piece falls on the family, to help loved ones prepare to pass away and, at the appropriate time, to actually encourage them by telling them it is okay to go.

The purpose of life is to attain salvation—to enter into everlasting life. That is our final "home." The purpose of marriage, for those who are married, is mutual salvation—for each spouse to help the other to attain salvation. And a family's ultimate gift to a loved one—grandparent, parent, spouse, friend, or, sadly, even a child—is to help them get safely "home" to the Kingdom of God. This help at some point will be the gentle nudge that it is okay to go to God. It is often at this point that the struggle ends and peaceful passing occurs.

The words of Psalm 130:5–6 are the words that ideally enter into the mind of someone who is at the end of life: "I wait for the LORD, my soul waits, and in his word I hope; / my soul waits for the LORD." These are words we should each pray during times of illness as we struggle to maintain patience and focus amid pain and discomfort. The words of a loving family could be a response to this psalm, saying to a loved one, "Go to the Lord, for whom you have been waiting so patiently."

> Let God arise, let his enemies be scattered;
> let those who hate him flee before him!
> As smoke is driven away, so drive them away;
> as wax melts before fire,
> let the wicked perish before God!
> But let the righteous be joyful;
> let them exult before God;
> let them be jubilant with joy!
> Sing to God, sing praises to his name;
> lift up a song to him who rides upon the clouds;
> His name is the LORD, exult before him.

Blessed be the LORD,
  who daily bears us up;
  God is our salvation.
Our God is a God of salvation;
  and to GOD, the Lord, belongs escape from death.
(Psalm 68:1–4, 19–20)

Let Them Know They Mattered

Therefore encourage one another and build one another up,
just as you are doing.

1 Thessalonians 5:11

I have spent a good deal of time writing about the topic of encouragement. Encouragement is something we all need; it is something we all can give. It is something that none of us gets enough of. We all deal with insecurities at times, and at times we all wonder, *Do I really matter to anyone?* and *Will anyone remember me when I'm gone?* These questions will keep us awake for many nights as we ponder the answers. It would be truly tragic if someone passed away from life with these thoughts. Here is how to make sure that doesn't happen.

The Gift of Encouragement

We've discussed offering our loved ones the gift of freedom, to have some control at the end of their lives. Another really important gift is the gift of encouragement, to let someone know that they truly mattered and will not be forgotten. "Thank you" and "you matter" are words we don't say, or hear, often enough. When we are close to people and around them all the time, we might be tempted to just assume they know how we feel about them—that we feel grateful for them, that we appreciate them, and that they have made an impact on us. We don't say these words enough to people when they are alive. In the stress that comes with the end of life, we might forget to say them. And the people who live with insecurities, which undoubtedly are magnified at the end with so much unknown and so much gone that makes life full, might actually be in their final stretch still wondering if their life really mattered.

Just about every eulogy at a funeral heaps praise on the person who has passed away. People say the nicest things in honoring the deceased. These occasions have often left me wondering, "Did you ever say all those nice things to your friend or family member when they were alive?"

Don't Wait to Speak Words of Encouragement

One of the most important people in my life was Fr. James Adams, who served as the dean of St. Sophia Cathedral in Los Angeles when I was in college. We had the conversation when I was 19, during my first confession, that totally changed the trajectory of my life. If that conversation hadn't occurred, I wouldn't be who I am today. Father James visited me in Florida many years ago, and I gave a sermon about how profoundly he had affected my life. I asked him to sit next to me while I was offering it. And I remember saying that we usually leave comments like this for a eulogy at a funeral. We don't always tell people in life exactly what they mean to us. I wanted Fr. James to know his significance to me, and I didn't want to wait for him to be gone before saying it. I wanted to say it to him directly.

Years later, Fr. James passed away, and I was honored to be a pallbearer at his funeral. He had been another father figure to me. Just in case you are wondering why it was so memorable, he is the priest who gave me a piece of advice when I was 19 and struggling with self-esteem. I had reached the point that I wondered if I mattered, and if I did, why was God allowing so many challenging things to happen in my life? He is the priest who told me, "Don't be a victim. Be a survivor. God wants survivors, not victims." In my life, that remains the single most life-altering thing anyone has ever said to me, and I find myself dispensing this advice to those to whom I offer counsel.

It's important to tell our loved ones what they mean to us while they are alive. It is important that we thank them. It is beneficial to offer them words of encouragement. It is comforting to let them know that they won't be forgotten. And it is especially important to give specific examples of what they did, why it mattered, and how it will be remembered.

Years ago at summer camp, we came up with an activity called "The Encouragement Walk," where we would choose someone and just rain down encouragement on them. One at a time, the people in their cabin—or, if we did this with a staff member, other members of the staff—would offer compliments, give encouragement, and express gratitude to this person. When it was over, the person receiving these words was on a real high. Everyone who received this gift of encouragement would be beaming when the experience was over. And those who had offered encouraging messages would be beaming also, because they had made someone else happy.

I've been on the receiving end of this exercise, and it feels great to know that we are appreciated, loved, and well thought of. I've also been on the giving end of this activity, and it feels just as satisfying to make someone else feel good, appreciated, loved, and well thought of. The only downside to this activity is that the high eventually wears off, and as we reenter normal life, with the joy of this activity becoming a distant memory.

What if an activity like this were someone's last experience? What if you poured out encouragement on your loved one in the last good moments of their life? They would leave this life with no doubt that they will be remembered and that they made a positive difference in the lives of others. They would be free from the insecurity that plagues each human and would leave this world with joy, confidence, and contentment.

Imagine that you were part of a family whose loved one was about to die, and as you said your good-byes, you were intentional about offering encouragement and thanks. Imagine how you would feel knowing that you helped bring joy, peace, confidence, and contentment to your loved one in their final moment. You would actually feel great, even in the midst of feeling sad.

Because the scene around someone who is dying frequently is stressful and chaotic, offering thanks and encouragement is often forgotten amid the frantic hope for just a little more time or some miraculous medical intervention. Again, some people will die suddenly, and others will linger in an unconscious state, but these situations are not as common. In most instances, there is a steady progression downward, and a family has opportunities to come together for a meaningful good-bye.

Imagine the people who mean the most to you all coming into your office or your home today to tell you how much you matter to them. This amazing thing would happen, then life would continue. Now imagine the people who mean the most to you coming into your room on your last day of life and sending you onward with these messages of thanks and love. You'd be able to leave this life and enter into eternal life in total peace. An infusion of encouragement would help with the "peaceful" part we all hope for in a painless, blameless, and peaceful end to a Christian life.

This specific reflection is the reason I wanted to write this book. If a family chooses to offer something like what has been described here, an intentional flood of encouragement for their loved one who is nearing death, they will have the peaceful ending we all pray for. Words of love will help a family to walk away with their own sense of contentment, that they offered a beautiful gift to a cherished loved one because they took time to say the things we all want to hear and don't hear enough of.

In working toward a painless, blameless, and peaceful exit from life, we have seen that medical personnel help with "painless," and the Church helps with the "blameless" part. Family and friends can do a lot to help with the "peaceful" part. An infusion of intentional encouragement and gratitude is an easy and effective way to provide this.

How lovely is thy dwelling place,
O LORD of hosts!
My soul longs, yea, faints
 for the courts of the LORD;
my heart and flesh sing for joy
 to the living God.

Even the sparrow finds a home
 and the swallow a nest for herself,
 where she may lay her young,
at thy altars, O LORD of Hosts,
 my King and My God.
Blessed are those who dwell in thy house,
 ever singing thy praise!

Blessed are the men whose strength is in thee,
 in whose heart are the highways of Zion.
As they go through the valley of Baca
 they make it a place of springs;
 the early rain also covers it with pools.
They go from strength to strength;
 the God of gods will be seen in Zion.

O Lord God of hosts, hear my prayer;
   give ear, O God of Jacob!
Behold our shield, O God;
   look upon the face of thine anointed!

For a day in thy courts is better
   than a thousand elsewhere.
I would rather be a doorkeeper in the house of my God
   then dwell in the tents of wickedness.
For the Lord God is a sun and shield;
   he bestows favor and honor.
No good thing does the Lord withhold
   from those who walk uprightly.
O Lord of hosts,
   blessed is the man who trusts in thee!
(Psalm 84)

We Don't Have Last Rites, but We Have a Last Prayer

Pray at all times in the Spirit, with all prayer and supplication.
Ephesians 6:18

Since so many people are uncomfortable talking about the end of life, it comes as no surprise that many people do not understand Orthodox practices surrounding death. The first misconception to clarify is to know that the Orthodox Church does not have "last rites." In the Catholic Church, the custom of "last rites" includes confession, a last Communion called "viaticum," and anointing with oil, called "extreme unction." But because many Catholics, like many Orthodox, wait to call a priest until someone has lost consciousness, often the last rites consist only of anointing and a prayer, as confession and Communion are no longer possible.[26]

Orthodox Prayers for Sickness and Death

In the Orthodox Church, the Sacraments of Holy Communion, Holy Unction, and Confession are available to all Orthodox at all times of life, especially when someone is very ill. We encourage those

---

26 Father Len Plazewski (Pastor of Christ the King Roman Catholic Church, Tampa, FL), in an interview with the author, January 29, 2024.

who are sick to avail themselves of these sacraments at any time, not only when circumstances become dire.

The Orthodox prayer book used by the priests, the *Efhologion*, has several prayers related to illness. One English version of the *Mikron Efhologion and Agiasmatarion: The Priest's Service Book*[27] contains prayers for those who are sick, a prayer for any illness, and prayers before and after an operation. These may be used throughout life as needed. The intention and petition of these prayers is for healing.

However, two specific prayers deal with the end of life, when healing is not possible. The first prayer is "For Those Suffering from Old Age or Incurable Illness." This prayer makes reference to "a Christian, painless, blameless, and peaceful end in faith and endurance" as well as "spiritual joy in the recollection of his/her good works." It asks the Lord to "lead him/her to repentance and confession of his/her trespasses; so that he/she may stand blameless before Your Son and our Lord and Savior Jesus Christ on the day of His second coming."[28]

The second prayer is called "Prayer at the Separation of the Soul from the Body." This prayer may be offered when death is imminent. It asks for the Lord to "bring about, in repose, the parting of the soul of your servant [Name] from his/her body." It literally asks God to end the person's life and take their soul from their body.

No Required Rituals

How are these prayers used in a practical way? First, there is no requirement that either of them be offered. If a person passes away and never had the prayer of the separation of soul and body offered over them, they didn't miss out on something essential for salvation.

---

27   Produced and translated by Fr. Evagoras Constantinides (Melissa Printing Company, 1989).
28   *Priest's Service Book*, 190–91.

Second, when making a pastoral visit at the end of a person's life, I explain to the family and to the patient, if they are conscious, the difference between the two prayers. One asks for strength as life ebbs away, and the other asks for life to end. I make sure before I offer a prayer, that this is indeed the prayer that is wanted. I wouldn't want to ask God to end a person's life if people were not okay with that. Third, the prayer of separation of soul and body is offered only when death is imminent—for instance, just before life support is disconnected or when vital signs indicate a person is actively dying.

It is really important to understand that there is no "need" for a priest to race to a hospital to get a prayer in before someone passes away. Yes, many times I do rush to the hospital, and in the case where the person has already passed, a Trisagion (memorial) service is offered, as the soul has already separated from the body. Also, there is no "need" for Holy Communion right at the end of life. If it is possible to offer someone Holy Communion, that is a blessing.

The prayers are there to aid us and those who are dying. But if we have lived a Christian life and have availed ourselves of the sacraments throughout life, receiving Holy Communion one more time at the end is not required. The fact that one has lived a Christ-centered life and is prepared to meet Him in death will bring more comfort to the one dying and to those left behind than one more frantic receiving of Holy Communion. And on the other side, one last ritual is not going to make up for the life that was not lived for Christ.

I love the LORD, because he has heard
    my voice and my supplications.
Because he inclined his ear to me,
    therefore I will call on him as long as I live.
The snares of death encompassed me;
    the pangs of Sheol laid hold on me;
    I suffered distress and anguish.

Then I called on the name of the LORD:
    "O LORD, I beseech thee, save my life!"

Gracious is the LORD, and righteous;
    our God is merciful.
The LORD preserves the simple;
    when I was brought low, he saved me.
Return, O my soul, to your rest;
    for the LORD has dealt bountifully with you.

For thou hast delivered my soul from death,
    my eyes from tears,
    my feet from stumbling;
I walk before the LORD
    in the land of the living.
I kept my faith, even when I said,
    "I am greatly afflicted";
I said in my consternation,
    "men are all a vain hope."

What shall I render to the LORD
    for all his bounty to me?
I will lift up the cup of salvation
    and call on the name of the LORD.
(Psalm 116:1–13)

I Want to Die with My Priest
at My Side—Fr. George

> Abraham breathed his last and died in a good old age, an old
> man and full of years, and was gathered to his people.
>
> Genesis 25:8

Father George was a retired priest who worshipped at St. John in Tampa during my first eighteen years there. He was a combination of Gandalf from *Lord of the Rings* and Confucius, with a long white beard and, in his later years, hunched over and carrying a cane. We affectionately called him "Yoda" because he was a wise old sage, like the Jedi creature from *Star Wars*. Many times he dispensed great advice, but he was also masterful at knowing when to stay quiet and let me find my own way. He became a good friend and confidant.

Father George was also a man of prayer and deep faith. He loved God. He loved people. And he loved serving God's people. He was at almost every service, usually choosing to sit in the very back pew of the church. He would write me notes in barely legible calligraphy. He didn't believe in email—everything he ever communicated in writing was handwritten, and only in his last years did he finally break down and get a cell phone.

"I Wouldn't Mind Dying in Church"

His health deteriorated slowly over time, but in his 90s Fr. George still drove a yellow "smart car" everywhere. We spoke often in his later years about death and heaven. He was not afraid of death. His only wish, however, was to outlive his wife, as he thought it was his duty to take care of her until the end. (He ended up passing before her.) One day I got a note from Fr. George which read, in part, "I wouldn't mind dying in church. However, if I die during a service, please don't stop the service; in fact, finish the service, grab lunch, and just call one of my children"—he left their numbers on the note—"at your convenience."

One day at our morning Bible study group, we were discussing John 5, the Gospel passage we read at funeral services, and the participants asked if I knew anyone who wasn't afraid to die. I answered without hesitation, "Father George." After Bible study, two of the participants were in my office talking, and I happened to see the note from Fr. George. I showed it to them so they could see I wasn't exaggerating.

The very next day, we celebrated Liturgy, and someone from Bible study was worshipping that morning. When I walked around the church for the Great Entrance, I noticed Fr. George sitting with his eyes closed and not moving, and I wondered if he had passed away. I walked slowly to see if his chest was moving, and it didn't appear to be. The person from Bible study noticed it too and sent me a text asking what was going on with Fr. George. It was an agonizing few minutes as I faced the altar table continuing the petitions of the Liturgy, wondering whether today was the day Fr. George would pass and if it really would happen in church. Fortunately, when I turned around to offer a blessing, Fr. George had opened his eyes, and we all breathed a sigh of relief.

A Prayer of Blessing at the End

A few weeks after this, Fr. George was in the hospital and was very ill. I visited him, and one of his daughters happened to be present. He told us that his dream was to pass away with me praying with him, with my hand on his head, blessing him as he took his last breath. I told Fr. George that this was a nice dream, and I thought to myself, "Like that will ever happen."

Turns out I was wrong.

One day, Fr. George's daughter asked if I could stop by his house. He wasn't doing particularly well. It wasn't a rush, she said—she just hoped I could come by sometime that day. I managed to find a free moment in the afternoon and went to the house. When I entered Fr. George's room, his eyes were closed. I said with enthusiasm, "Hi, Father George, it's Father Stavros. I came to see you today." His daughter had told me he hadn't been responsive all day, so I didn't expect an answer. However, to my surprise, Fr. George opened his eyes and stared at me.

I looked at him and asked quietly, "Is today the day for the prayer you dreamed of?"

He nodded his head and closed his eyes. I began to pray the prayer of the separation of soul and body. (See previous reflection.) I placed my hand on top of Fr. George's head and made the sign of the cross. As my hand rested on his head ever so briefly, he let out one breath—and then there was nothing. I could see his cheeks fall almost immediately, and I knew that he had passed.

I stopped praying, looked at the nurse, and said almost flippantly, "I think he just died." To be honest, I was shocked that this man's dream had come true. She put the stethoscope to his chest for a few moments and confirmed that he had passed away.

I slid my hand from his head and got on my knees, as I always do when someone dies—a sign of respect for the angels who fill the room to take the soul from the body and carry it to God. After a few minutes of silence, I got up and offered a Trisagion for Fr. George. And as I left the house sometime later, I called a friend and said, "I had the *privilege* to watch Fr. George pass away today." Because indeed it was a privilege—a blessing to see not only a good friend but a solid Christian man take his last breath on earth and begin his journey home to God, and to do it as the fulfillment of a dream he prayed would come true.

Memory eternal, Fr. George!

The LORD is my shepherd, I shall not want;
    he makes me lie down in green pastures.
He leads me beside still waters;
    he restores my soul.
He leads me in the paths of righteousness
    for his name's sake.

Even though I walk through the valley of the shadow of death,
    I fear no evil;
for thou art with me;
    thy rod and thy staff,
    they comfort me.

Thou preparest a table before me
    in the presence of my enemies;
thou anointest my head with oil,
    my cup overflows.
Surely goodness and mercy shall follow me
    all the days of my life;
and I shall dwell in the house of the LORD
    for ever.
(Psalm 23)

At the Moment of Death
and Afterward

There Are Angels Among Us

The poor man died and was carried by the angels to
Abraham's bosom.

Luke 16:22

In this section of the book, we will focus on the moment of death
and what happens afterward. There are lots of pious people who
have made theological comment on what happens after we die. To
this day, different ideas are discussed, some of which create confu-
sion as well as provide comfort.

My thoughts on death and what happens afterward are taken
only from the Bible, which in some ways provides a framework but
leaves out the details of how things specifically happen. As an example, the instructions for the Eucharist, as revealed in the Bible, are
very simple. Jesus tells us that we are to partake often of His flesh
and blood (John 6:53–58) in the form of bread and wine, which are
the Body and Blood of Christ (Luke 22:19–20), and that we should
do so with preparation (1 Cor. 11:27–30). The method by which we
receive Holy Communion, as well as our preparation and our service
of the Divine Liturgy, evolved over centuries and has been codified
through Holy Tradition and canon law so that it is done the same
way over all the world.

Because there is, to my knowledge, no universal teaching about what exactly happens when we die, other than what is universally accepted in the sacred Scriptures, we will begin reflecting on what happens at death and after death by examining what we know from the Bible.

What Happens at the Moment of Death

Earlier we discussed the Parable of the Rich Man and Lazarus,[29] as told in the Gospel of Luke 16:19–31. In this reflection, we will focus on just one verse of that parable that we have not yet discussed. In the parable, Jesus reveals to us that "the poor man died and was carried by the angels to Abraham's bosom." We know that our earthly bodies decay; they do not leave this world and go anywhere. Rather, the soul, which is an unquantifiable part of our bodies, leaves and goes to the Lord. This is facilitated by the angels.

"Unquantifiable"—what does that mean? There are many aspects of human beings that can be measured scientifically and medically: our height, weight, the state of our organs, and our vital signs. A determination can be made positively that a person has died, because the things that need to happen in the body in order for us to be alive have stopped. Physical health and health failing to the point that death has occurred are quantifiable.

Then there is the state of our minds, our mental health. We can take aptitude tests to quantify what the mind knows—a math test can determine whether someone knows how to add and subtract, as an example. Personality tests can indicate whether one leans toward being an introvert or an extrovert—although it would be hard to say that one person is twice as introverted as someone else, because this trait can't be measured in a quantifiable way like weight or height.

---

29   See "It's Too Late After We Die—The Rich Man and Lazarus" on page 99.

Each person has two qualities that are unquantifiable—a sparkle in their eye, and a *prosopon*. This is a Greek word which can mean the face of a person, or their countenance. While a face is quantifiable, with physical features like eyes, nose, and mouth, the "countenance" is harder to quantify. The countenance is the essence of a person. The absence of certain physical traits, like heartbeat or brainwaves, indicate that a person is not alive, but the unquantifiable traits also cease. That sparkle in the eye is gone and the countenance is gone: The essence of the person is gone.

I have been present many times when a person has passed away. I can tell when death occurs not just because of the machines that monitor vitals, but by looking at someone. I can see the countenance fall: The color leaves the face, and the essence of that person disappears. And at the moment of death, as all these things cease, the soul departs from the body and is carried by the angels to the Lord, according to Luke 16:22.

In the Presence of the Angels

When a passing is not sudden and traumatic—in other words, when a person just quietly slips out of life—I have generally found the moment of death to be both peaceful and powerful. I've sensed the presence of others in the room at that moment, and the "others" who are unquantifiable are the angels. Any time I am in the room at the end of life, my natural inclination is to get on my knees and just be silent, and in some sense to "enjoy" the presence of the angels. I think in these moments of Moses in Exodus 3:2–5, where we read:

> And the angel of the LORD appeared to him in a flame of fire out of the midst of a bush; and he looked, and lo, the bush was burning, yet it was not consumed. And Moses said, "I will turn aside and see this great sight, why the bush is not burnt." When

the LORD saw that he turned aside to see, God called to him out of the bush, "Moses, Moses!" And he said, "Here am I." Then he said, "Do not come near; put off your shoes from your feet, for the place on which you are standing is holy ground."

At the time of death, I've been privileged to be in the room with people I liked, people who were my friends, people whose passing saddened me, and people whom I truly loved, truly miss, and truly mourned. But at *the moment* of death, I have never been overcome by a sense of sadness. That comes later. Instead, I have been overwhelmed by a sense of holiness, that the ground on which we were standing was holy ground because the angels of God were on it with us.

For those who have never seen someone pass away and are wondering what it is like, this is what it is like for me. I pray that the prospect of seeing this will leave you hopeful and not anxious. If you have seen someone pass away, undoubtedly that was someone that you may still be mourning. Take comfort that you were present on the holy ground, shared with the angels.

> I have done what is just and right;
> > do not leave me to my oppressors.
> But surety for thy servant for good;
> > let not the godless oppress me.
> My eyes fail with watching for thy salvation,
> > and for the fulfillment of thy righteous promise.
> Deal with thy servant according to thy steadfast love,
> > and teach me thy statues.
> I am thy servant; give me understanding,
> > that I may know thy testimonies!
> It is time for the LORD to act,
> > for thy law has been broken.

Therefore I love thy commandments
    above gold, above fine gold.
Therefore I direct my steps by all thy precepts;
    I hate every false way.
(Ps. 119:121–128)

Faithful to the End—Anastasia

But he who endures to the end will be saved.

Matthew 24:13

Anastasia was a health nut. She was always in the gym, running, and watching what she ate. She was the last person one would have thought would pass away at age 53. It is paradoxical that some people who seem to do everything right from a health perspective die at a young age, while some who seem to do everything wrong from a health perspective live to be very old.

Anastasia came to the office one day and told me she had just been diagnosed with stage-four colon cancer. The prognosis was not good. In the course of our conversation, she told me, "No matter what happens, I will not blame or curse God. I will remain faithful to the end." This was in October 2014.

Over the course of the next fifteen months, she had many treatments, many of which were painful and invasive. She never complained. And she tried, as best as she could, to keep on living—she kept coming to Bible study, kept coming to church, and of course she kept being a mom to her five children and a wife to her husband.

In my parish, we have a custom on Pascha that the light of Christ is given to three women to distribute to the congregation, in remembrance of the myrrhbearing women who went to the empty Tomb at the Resurrection. The name *Anastasia* means "resurrection," and the Greek word for resurrection is *anastasis*. On Pascha 2015, Anastasia was one of the three women who were given this honor. She wrote me a letter the next day, articulating that at the moment she received the light, she felt like she was in heaven, and that if this is what heaven was like, she was not worried about dying anymore.

Preparing While We Still Have Time

Fast forward to December 2015. The treatments had become ineffective, and it looked like Anastasia didn't have much time to live. In mid-December, I went and visited her at home. I considered her a friend, and it was hard to see a friend going through what she was suffering. Like all her friends, I was rooting for her to pull through and beat the cancer. But as a priest, I knew that we needed to have a difficult conversation because it didn't seem that recovery was going to happen.

I remember we started off talking about miracles—that two kinds of miracles were at play. One would be the miracle of beating cancer. The other would be the miracle of God opening the gates of heaven and letting her enter them. She would get a miracle, one way or the other. I told her, in words that were difficult to say to a friend, "You know that the treatments are not working and that you are going to die very shortly. Deep down you know that. I know that. And now it is time to start preparing for that." It was very hard to say these words. I did not want her to die.

After a few moments of silence, she looked at me and said, "You are right. I know that I don't have much time. I probably should make an appointment to see you for confession before I die."

I replied, "We don't know how much time you have—it could be any time. We should do confession today, right here."

She thought about that for a moment and said, "Okay, give me a few minutes to collect my thoughts."

And then she went to confession on the back porch of her home. I don't remember anything of that conversation, as I never remember those details—only that she felt a lot better when we were finished. The lesson here is that when death is imminent, we should take time to prepare while there is still time to prepare.

Final Wishes

A few weeks later, on New Year's Eve, Anastasia's family asked me to stop by the house to ask her about her wishes for her funeral. They didn't want her to think they were giving up on her, but they also didn't know where she wanted to be buried. We had a conversation, and she made her wishes known and told her family. It was a very mature conversation that many people feel uncomfortable initiating or having. When we were done with that, I asked her if she wanted anything specific for her funeral.

She remembered a funeral from a few years before, when a friend of ours named Marilyn had passed away fairly young. Marilyn had sung in the choir, and before her funeral we celebrated the Divine Liturgy with the choir. Anastasia was at that funeral, and she said, "I want you to do for me what you did for Marilyn. I want there to be Liturgy. I want the choir to sing. And I want everyone to walk out of the church and say, 'Wow.'"

Then she asked me, "When you get up there and talk about me, what are you going to say?"

I replied, "I'm going to say that you were faithful to the end."

The last week of Anastasia's life saw a steady decline. One week before she passed, she was still walking, eating, and even cooking. Five days before her death at home, when I visited her, she walked me to the door, but with great difficulty. At three days before, she couldn't walk anymore. I visited her again, and we said our goodbyes. It seemed like her passing would be any time.

Anastasia told me that she wanted me to be in her house when she died so that I could comfort her family, and that she would wait for me to get there. The day before she passed, it was a Saturday, and we couldn't figure out how she was still living, as all her vital signs were failing. I had a thought that God would send His angels for her at the hour of the Resurrection, for her personal *anastasi*, and that she would pass after the Sabbath was over and before the sun rose on Sunday. Her family knew of her wish for me to be present when she passed, and I told them that if she passed in the middle of the night, to call me. If she didn't pass in the middle of the night, that I would be there at 7:00 a.m. since the sunrise was 7:30 a.m. that Sunday.

Anastasia Gets Her Wish

I arrived at her home at 7:00 a.m. on Sunday, January 17, 2016. I went into the room, and my first thought was, "Dear God, this has gone on long enough." She looked emaciated, almost like a ghost. I stepped out of the room to greet her family, and then we went back into the room together.

In those two minutes when no one was in the room, she passed away. As we looked at her, moments after her passing, her entire countenance had changed. Her head had turned from the left to the right, and she was looking toward the window and smiling. She transformed from looking like an emaciated ghost to looking beautiful again. Of course, everyone was in tears that she had died, but someone noticed her smile.

I said, "It's like she looked out the window and saw the angels coming for her, and she is happy." We all got on our knees respectfully because the moment of death for a faithful person is a holy moment. Angels enter the room, and we should be appropriately reverent.

Anastasia's funeral was held the following Friday. Our church was full, and so was the hall. Anastasia knew a *lot* of people, and a lot of people loved her. Because Anastasia had lived her whole life in South Tampa, she was well known in that tight-knit community.

The choir sang a beautiful Divine Liturgy, and the funeral followed. Most of the people in attendance were not Orthodox. To this day, I run into people in South Tampa who recognize me as Anastasia's priest, and they still say, "I remember you from Anastasia's funeral. Wow!"

She got her wish. As for my eulogy, it ended with the words, "Anastasia was faithful to the end." Indeed, she was.

Sometimes the miracle is not the miracle of healing but the miracle of eternal life, which we believe comes by God's grace to those who remain faithful to the end.

Memory eternal, Anastasia!

Deliver me from my enemies, O my God,
    protect me from those who rise up against me,
deliver me from those who work evil,
    and save me from bloodthirsty men.

For lo, they lie wait for my life;
    fierce men band themselves against me.
For no transgression or sin of mine, O Lord,
    for no fault of mine, they run and make ready.

Rouse thyself, come to my help, and see!
    Thou, Lord God of hosts, art God of Israel.
Awake to punish all the nations;
    spare none of those who treacherously plot evil.

Each evening they come back,
 howling like dogs
 and prowling about the city.
There they are, bellowing with their mouths,
 and snarling with their lips—
 for "Who," they think, "will hear us?"

But thou, O LORD, dost laugh at them;
 thou dost hold all the nations in derision.
O my Strength, I will sing praises to thee;
 for thou, O God, art my fortress.
My God in His steadfast love will meet me;
 my God will let me look in triumph on my enemies.

Slay them not, lest my people forget;
 make them totter by thy power, and bring them down,
 O LORD, our shield!
For the sin of their mouths, the words of their lips,
 let them be trapped in their pride.
For the cursing and lies which they utter,
 consume them in wrath,
 consume them till they are no more,
that men may know that God rules over Jacob
 to the ends of the earth.

Each evening they come back,
 howling like dogs
 and prowling about the city.
They roam about for food,
 and growl if they do not get their fill.

But I will sing of thy might;
   I will sing aloud of thy steadfast love in the morning.
For thou hast been to me a fortress
   and a refuge in the day of my distress.
O my Strength, I will sing praises to thee,
   for thou, O God, art my fortress,
     the God who shows me steadfast love.
(Psalm 59)

Pastoral Guidelines Concerning
Issues Related to Death

Greater love has no man than this, that a man lay down his life
for his friends.

John 15:13

Because speaking about death is uncomfortable for many people, we either don't know or don't share certain things that we
should know as Orthodox Christians. We will discuss several of
these in this section. A lot could be said on each subject, but this will
serve as a summary. The first issue concerns whether organ donation
is acceptable.

Organ Donation

The *2020 Yearbook* of the Greek Orthodox Archdiocese of America
provides pastoral guidelines regarding organ donation written by the
late Fr. Stanley Harakas, who was widely recognized for teaching
and writing on Orthodox ethical issues. He writes:

> Although nothing in the Orthodox tradition requires the
> faithful to donate their organs to others, nevertheless, this
> practice may be considered an act of love, and as such is

encouraged. The decision to donate a duplicate organ, such as a kidney, while the donor is living, requires much consideration and should be made in consultation with medical professionals and one's Spiritual Father. The donation of an organ from a deceased person is also an act of love that offers the recipient a longer, fuller life. Such donations are acceptable if the deceased donor had willed such action, or if surviving relatives permit it, providing that it was in harmony with the desires of the deceased. Such actions can be approved as an expression of love and the self-determination of the donor. In all cases, respect for the body of the donor should be maintained. Organ transplants should not be commercialized nor coerced nor take place without proper consent, nor place in jeopardy the identity of the donor or recipient, through, for example, the use of animal organs. The death of the donor should never be hastened in order to harvest organs for transplantation to another person.[30]

Because we are created by God Himself in His image and likeness, we have dignity and infinite value. If we can extend the life of someone else by giving them organs we won't need after we die, this gift acknowledges that we value others—so much so that we believe in offering a gesture of love and caring to extend their lives, even as our own life ends (though we do not hasten our death in order to accomplish this).

Cremation

Father Harakas again offers the Orthodox view on this subject when he writes,

---

30   *2020 Yearbook* (Greek Orthodox Archdiocese of America, 2020), 268.

Because the Orthodox Faith affirms the fundamental goodness of creation, it understands the body to be an integral part of the human person and the temple of the Holy Spirit, and expects the resurrection of the dead. The Church considers cremation to be the deliberate desecration and destruction of what God has made and ordained for us. The Church instead insists that the body be buried so that the natural physical process of decomposition may take place. The Church does not grant funerals, either in the sanctuary, or at the funeral home, or at any other place, to persons who have chosen to be cremated.[31]

Part of this teaching on the importance of burial comes from Ezekiel 37, a vision of the future resurrection of all people, where the prophet comes upon a valley of dry bones—not ashes—and the bones come together into a new creation with new bodies and new breath. In addition to this biblical teaching, we have the burial of Christ Himself, whose physical body was laid in the grave.[32]

Is cremation going to send someone to eternal condemnation? That is not our call. What about bodies that have burned in a fire, or been lost, or buried at sea? These are extremes. What we are reflecting on here is the traditional practice of the Church and expectation of her members.

There are many aspects of Church practice where *economia,* or dispensation, is given when what is expected cannot or does not happen. Cremation is not such an instance. The only exception to this would be first by consent of a bishop, and second, in an extreme circumstance, such as a city running out of cemetery space and enacting a civil law that burial is not allowed within a municipality. For

---

31   *2020 Yearbook,* 268.
32   For a more thorough discussion of cremation, burial, and Church Tradition, see the Ancient Faith Topical Series booklet, *Cremation: An Orthodox View* (Ancient Faith Publishing, 2025).

example, Orthodox Christians in Japan are cremated because the law requires cremation, but a church funeral is performed beforehand.[33] This is the only kind of extenuating circumstance where cremation would be allowed.

Sometimes very pious people cannot afford a traditional burial. This situation should be discussed before a death occurs, within the local community and with the presiding hierarch.

Open Casket

Sometimes mourners are surprised by the opening of a casket at an Orthodox funeral service. It is the position of the Church that there is dignity to the human body. It is to be honored in life and in death. The Tradition of the Orthodox Church is that a casket be open at a funeral service to honor the remains of the deceased and to confirm the finality of death. Seeing a loved one after they have passed helps to bring closure, as we then have seen them both in life and in death. It also helps us deal with the reality of death.

The Church does not offer a closed casket with a photo collection and a "celebration of life," but instead provides a tangible confirmation that we are dealing with a death and all the appropriate emotions that accompany it, including grief. Again, there are extenuating circumstances when an open casket would not be required, such as significant trauma to the body of the deceased.

Assisted Suicide

Euthanasia, sometimes called assisted suicide or "mercy killing," is now legal in many places, but the Church cannot endorse this action.

---

33   "Deaths/Funerals," The Orthodox Faith: Questions & Answers, *Orthodox Church in America*, https://www.oca.org/questions/deathfunerals.

We believe first in the mercies of God. We've already discussed that it is not our role to choose when life ends. This decision belongs to God alone, who is the Author of life. While discontinuing a medical treatment and letting "nature take its course" is ethical (as we discussed earlier in the "Tough End-of-Life Decisions" section, beginning on page 105), deliberately ending life is not.

We have discussed the intentional will and the permissive will of God. God may intentionally extend someone's time on earth in order for them to repent and prepare for death. He may permit suffering for the same reason. This is why faith is important. We cannot know that mind of God, or His exact intention in either intending or allowing something to happen. By deliberately ending life, it is as if we have put ourselves into the mind of God and have ourselves made the decision for an ending, neither letting nature take its course nor allowing the will of God to play out. Faith is the ability to trust in the unknown, and changing what is unknown to something we knowingly control contradicts the idea of faith.

Embalming

The Church does not prohibit embalming the body of the deceased because in some instances, many days lapse between a death and the gathering of the family for the funeral. Strictly speaking, a body should naturally return to its elements, and embalming slows this process down. It is not required but not prohibited.

Death by Suicide

Finally, the last issue concerns burial for those who have died by suicide. Generally speaking, a funeral is allowed if the deceased can be shown to have been under psychological or psychiatric care for mental illness—in others words, the person was known not to be in the proper frame of mind to make rational decisions.[34] In every Ortho-dox jurisdiction, the decision is the bishop's. It is common for some to make an allowance for a funeral if the person was known to be mentally ill and did not kill themselves out of a principled or ideolog-ical belief in suicide. Ultimately, however, the judgment of the bishop is what makes the determination.

In most instances now, it is presumed that no one in their right mind would make a decision to terminate their life. Thus, whether the person is being treated for a mental illness or experiences a tem-porary episode that leads to suicide, in every instance I have heard of, a hierarch will grant permission for a funeral to be held. In the several deaths by suicide that have happened in my ministry, my hierarch has always granted permission. His only request was that the individual's priest inform him of the circumstances and ask his permission, then he offered his blessing.

It is important to talk about Orthodox practices and teachings concerning death so that we are familiar with them before someone passes away. The period of grief and mourning surrounding a death is not the best time to make important decisions—or to be surprised by the Church's traditions. It is good to understand and to plan well before this situation presents itself.

> Thy testimonies are wonderful;
>   therefore my soul keeps them.
> The unfolding of thy words gives light;
>   it imparts understanding to the simple.
> With open mouth I pant,
>   because I long for thy commandments.
> Turn to me and be gracious to me,
>   as is thy wont toward those who love thy name.

---

34 *2020 Yearbook*, 269.

Keep steady my steps according to thy promise,
and let no iniquity get dominion over me.
Redeem me from man's oppression,
that I may keep thy precepts.
Make thy face shine upon thy servant,
and teach me thy statutes.
My eyes shed streams of tears,
because men do not keep thy law.
(Psalm 119:129–136)

Meaningful Closure

Let us then with confidence draw near to the throne of grace,
that we may receive mercy and find grace to help in time
of need.

Hebrews 4:16

This reflection offers some ideas of practical and meaningful things to do when someone has passed away. First of all, it is necessary in all instances that a person be pronounced dead by medical personnel. This happens in a hospital or hospice facility. If someone passes at home, this practice still will be necessary. The person who makes the official pronouncement could be a hospice nurse, a paramedic, or other medical workers.

Procedures for Taking Care of the Body After Death

When death occurs, it will be necessary to call a funeral home to come and take the body of the deceased to prepare them for burial.[35] If a

---

35 Not all states require the participation of a licensed funeral director when a death occurs. Some Orthodox churches in the US have formed burial societies, and members of the parish take care of arrangements. For more information on this ancient practice of caring for the dead, see the book, *A Christian Ending: Rediscovering Ancient Christian Burial Customs for the Modern World*, by Dn. Mark Barna (Divine Ascent Press, 2018), or listen to

person or a family has not preplanned with a funeral home, calling them and signing over the body of a deceased loved one might be seen as an implied contract to work with that funeral home. If the family visits the funeral home a few hours later and is shocked to learn how much they charge for services, it might be difficult to have the remains transferred to a different funeral home. A practical piece of advice: When a loved one is well up in years, very sick, or death is imminent, preplanning for a funeral while not under duress is a good idea.

When the funeral home staff arrive to remove a loved one from a home or hospital, it is customary—and in many instances required— that their body be completely covered for removal and transport to a funeral home or other place of preparation. We all have many memories of our loved ones coming in and out of their home; this image of them being covered and taken away is a memory that none of us needs to have. I advise families to step into another room when the personnel come to take the remains of their loved one out of the house for the last time.

Working with Funeral Home and Parish

The funeral home staff will need biographical information in order to process a death certificate, so have information at the ready such as a mother's maiden name and social security number—facts we might not know. Secondly, the staff will want a complete set of clothing to dress your loved one, including undergarments and shoes. Try to make only one trip to the funeral home, since a visit can be traumatic, and make sure you take all the clothes that are needed.

The process for circulating obituaries by a funeral home or news source varies from place to place. It can be helpful to think of the

---

the Ancient Faith podcast of the same name.

information one would want presented in an obituary even before death occurs so that it doesn't have to be written under the stress of grief and the duress of having to get a lot of things done within a short period of time. Using pallbearers is a nice tradition, where people who have been meaningful in the life of the person who has passed bear their casket. This is certainly preferable to paying funeral home staff to do it. Usually six to eight pallbearers is the appropriate number.

Because of the coordination needed between funeral home, cemetery, and church, it may take several days to schedule a funeral. As you plan, it's also important to note that the Orthodox Church does not allow family members to speak in church at a funeral. In the metropolis where I currently serve, we encourage those who want to speak to do so at a wake or a viewing (a more intimate gathering of family and perhaps close friends) the night before, or at the "mercy meal" after the funeral.

Neither a wake, a viewing, nor a makaria ("mercy meal") are required by the Church. Wakes and viewings generally take place at a funeral home the night before a funeral. The atmosphere is casual, and the time allotted is longer than a funeral, allowing loved ones to gather in fellowship and converse about the deceased while consoling one another.

A makaria is served after the funeral, and people can again gather in fellowship. It is generally held at the church hall, a restaurant, or in the home of a family member of the deceased. Typically fish is served because after the Resurrection, Jesus shared a meal of bread and fish with His disciples (John 21:1–13).

Practical Ideas

In over twenty-five years as a priest, I've picked up a lot of practical ideas, especially concerning death. Here are a few more.

+ Ask the funeral home for a private family viewing so that close family members have some personal time with the deceased before the public comes in. Ask family members, even adults, to write personal letters to the deceased. This is particularly good for children, to write or draw something for a grandparent, but it is something even adult children can do for their parent. The letter-writing gives people something to do and something to focus on. Put together a package of letters, drawings, and a family photo, and place them in the casket during the private viewing.

+ Part of the Orthodox funeral service requires the priest to place oil and earth over the body of the deceased at the end of the service. Many priests take sand from the candle stand in the church for this purpose, since it is readily available. At one funeral years ago, a family brought in a bunch of things from the home of the deceased to place in the casket, such as golf balls and a TV remote control, so that the person who had died could "have some of their things." I found this a little disrespectful, actually, but it spawned an idea: Why not bring something from their home that is actually needed? Since that time, I have asked families to bring me a bag of dry dirt from the home of the deceased, and I place this earth on the body at the end of the funeral. If this is something you want to do, ask your priest about it.

+ People have brought icons that are family heirlooms to be buried with the deceased. I don't like the idea of parting with valuable things that should stay in a family. Instead, we have small paper icons that we place in the hand of the deceased. The icon that is printed by the funeral home for funeral services also can suffice if you want to bury an icon with a loved one.

+ Finally, each of us carries an infinite number of images of a loved one in our minds. As I suggested earlier that family members not watch the funeral home personnel cover up a loved one, I also humbly suggest not watching the lid of the casket close for the final time. I remember attending a funeral before I was ordained where the lid slammed with a loud thud. It made people jump and become emotional. I always try to get in the way when the lid is closed so that the family does not see this. At my own parents' funerals, I just turned away and didn't watch. There is no need to hold that image in our minds.

Deaths and funerals are traumatic events in our lives. Hopefully these practical ideas will make some of these experiences a little bit easier.

Righteous art thou, O LORD,
    and right are thy judgments.
Thou has appointed thy testimonies in righteousness
    and in all faithfulness.
My zeal consumes me,
    because my foes forget thy words.
Thy promise is well tried,
    and thy servant loves it.
I am small and despised,
    yet I do not forget thy precepts.
Thy righteousness is righteous forever,
    and thy law is true.
Trouble and anguish have come upon me,
    but thy commandments are my delight.
Thy testimonies are righteous forever;
    give me understanding that I may live.
(Psalm 119:137–144)

The Funeral Service

Have Mercy on Me

Turn to me and be gracious to me,
as is thy wont toward those who love thy name.

Psalm 119:132

We turn now our attention to the funeral service. Much of it was written by St. John of Damascus in the 700s, and this brilliant composition has not been changed in centuries. The service includes a plea for mercy on behalf of the deceased, some education for those who are mourning as well as contemplating their own deaths, two thought-provoking Scripture readings, and a beautiful farewell hymn, "Memory Eternal." It also contains several meaningful rituals. We will spend the next several reflections discussing the funeral service and both the comfort and thought it provides for those who are grieving.

Bringing the Deceased into the Church

When the body of the deceased is brought to the church, the priest meets the casket at the door of the narthex and offers incense over it before it is brought into the church. When I think of this ritual, I am reminded of icons of the Theotokos that depict her sitting on a throne holding the Christ child, with angels on each side offering incense. I also think of an angel standing at the gate of heaven offering incense over the soul of the newly departed. It is a comforting thought.

Allow me to share in a personal way that one of my toughest tasks as a priest is to walk down the aisle before a funeral to meet the casket in the narthex. The phrase "walking down the aisle" usually evokes the image of a bride at her wedding, where she lingers on her walk, soaking in the moment. My experience at a funeral is totally the opposite. I move down the aisle quickly because it is always a lonely and sad walk, even for the people who are old and have lived a long and full life. It is especially difficult when I make that trip for a friend.

Our Account Before the Lord

The funeral service begins with the singing of three groups of six verses, each from Psalm 119.[36] This psalm is written in the first person, so as we sing these verses, it is as if we are singing them on behalf of the deceased and in anticipation of our own death and account before the Lord.

It is important to remember that each of us will have an accounting before the Lord. The Bible states this very clearly. He will be the judge of who inherits His Kingdom and who does not. Much as it is tempting to place a person in heaven in our thoughts, that decision rests with the Lord. There are many people I have met, some of whom I have written about in this book, whom I considered to be righteous. I would like to think that they are in heaven. I think that if they are not in heaven, I certainly won't be. But to place someone in heaven, or in hell, belongs to the Lord and not to us.

Admitting someone into heaven is an act of mercy on the part of God. In Romans 6:23 we read, "For the wages of sin is death, but the

---

36 Psalm 119 has 176 verses, and in certain Orthodox jurisdictions, all of them are sung. The Greek Orthodox funeral service uses only eighteen of them.

free gift of God is eternal life in Christ Jesus our Lord." Because we all sin, we all deserve death—separation from God and also physical death. Eternal life is a gift from God, one that He offers freely. We "owe" death because of our sins, and none of us is worthy to "claim" heaven. Thus, we plead for the mercy of God, for Him to overlook the "wages" we deserve for our sins and instead to offer us mercy and the free gift of eternal life.

Having officiated at hundreds of funerals, I am cognizant that one day, there will be a funeral for me. I will need God's mercies because I sin, just like everyone else, and the wages of my sins are my physical death. Yet, we believe in the mercies of God, and so we pray for them on behalf of the deceased and in anticipation of our own death.

There is a beautiful icon called "Christ the merciful judge." The original is found in the Monastery of St. Katherine on Mount Sinai, and each of Christ's eyes is painted differently. If you cover the left side of Christ's face, you will see that the right side has a look of serenity and peace. If you cover the right side, you will see that the left side has a look of both anger and sadness. We know that we will stand in judgment before Christ. We know that He is merciful. Just how merciful and how judging He will be is unknown. But we believe in the power of prayer.

We Are Members of the Church, in Life and in Death

We believe that we will always be part of the Church. Allow me to introduce two terms—the "Church Militant" and the "Church Triumphant." The Church Militant is the fighting Church on earth—those who are alive and are in the spiritual struggle. The Church Triumphant is the one in heaven—those who have passed on. We will always belong to the Church—either the Church Militant or the Church Triumphant. Thus, we pray for those who are no longer part of the Church Militant, and so it is appropriate for us to pray for the mercy of God over the person who has left our company. They may have ceased living on earth, but that does not make them a nonentity. Each of us has a soul that will live eternally.

> Bless the LORD, O my soul;
> and all that is within me, bless his holy name!
> Bless the LORD, O my soul,
>   and forget not all his benefits,
> who forgives all your iniquity,
>   who heals all your diseases,
> who redeems your life from the Pit,
>   who crowns you with steadfast love and mercy,
> who satisfies you with good as long as you live,
>   so that your youth is renewed like the eagle's.

> The LORD works vindication
>   and justice for all who are oppressed.
> He made known his ways to Moses,
>   his acts to the people of Israel.
> The LORD is merciful and gracious,
>   slow to anger and abounding in steadfast love.
> He will not always chide,
>   nor will he keep his anger forever.
> He does not deal with us according to our sins,
>   nor requite us according to our iniquities.
> For as the heavens are high above the earth,
>   so great is his steadfast love toward those who fear him;
> as far as the east is from the west,
>   so far does he remove our transgressions from us.
> As a father pities his children,
>   so the Lord pities those who fear him.
> For he knows our frame;
>   he remembers that we are dust.

As for man, his days are like grass;
 he flourishes like a flower of the field;
for the wind passes over it, and it is gone,
 and its place knows it no more.
But the steadfast love of the LORD is from everlasting to
 everlasting
  upon those who fear him,
 and his righteousness to children's children,
to those who keep his covenant
 and remember to do his commandments.

The Lord has established his throne in the heavens,
 and his kingdom rules over all.
Bless the LORD, O you his angels,
 you mighty ones who do his word,
 hearkening to the voice of his word!
Bless the LORD, all his hosts,
 his ministers that do his will!
Bless the LORD, all his works,
 in all places of his dominion.
Bless the LORD, O my soul!
(Psalm 103)

Among the Saints

The memory of the righteous is a blessing.

Proverbs 10:7

Precious in the sight of the LORD is the death of his saints.

Psalm 116:15

After the first three stasis, or stanzas, of Psalm 119, the funeral service continues with the *evlogitaria*, a set of hymns that each begin with the verse, "Blessed are You, O Lord; teach me Your commandments." These may sound familiar, as they are part of the memorial services we hear so often after the Divine Liturgy and during Orthros, or Matins. The first three of these hymns are also written in the first person. We sing these on behalf of the deceased and in anticipation of our own exit from this life. The words are appropriate both for the one who has passed and for us who remain to ponder. Here are a few of the verses:[37]

I am the lost sheep: O Savior, call me back and save me.

---

37   This and the following quotations from "Sacraments and Blessings: Funeral," PDF text in English, 2-3. From the *Digital Chant Stand* of the Greek Orthodox Archdiocese, https://dcs.goarch.org.

Lead me back again to Your likeness, so that the ancient beauty may be refashioned.

Grant me the desired homeland for which I long, making me again a citizen of Paradise.

The fourth hymn moves to the third person, referring specifically to the deceased and asking God to "place him/her in Paradise where the choirs of the Saints and the righteous, O Lord, will shine as the stars of heaven."[38] The hymnographer uses such vivid imagery. I have always described the stars as majestic, and to be part of God's majesty is such a comforting thought, especially for the family left behind—that their loved one is sharing in God's majesty.

The next hymns return to the plural, asking God to "illumine us who worship You in faith and deliver us from the eternal fire." The sixth and final hymn of this set is addressed to the Theotokos, asking, "Through you, pure and blessed Theotokos, may we find Paradise." While it is the Lord who ultimately will grant us admission to Paradise, we have the Theotokos, the Ever-Virgin Mary, as both example and intercessor on our behalf.

A Beloved Hymn

One of the more well-known hymns of the funeral and memorial services follows, as we sing "With the Saints, give rest, O Christ, to the soul of Your servant where there is no pain, no sorrow, no sighing, but life everlasting." Traditionally the priest will offer incense over the body of the deceased at this point. There are several takeaways from this hymn.

---

38 "Sacraments and Blessings: Funeral," 3.

+ **Connection with the saints.** The word for "saint" in Greek is *agios*, which can be translated "set apart." A saint is someone whose life was distinguished because it was set apart for God. In this instance, we are also praying that God will set our loved one in the ranks of the saints—all those who have pleased God and who have been deemed worthy by Him to enter into His heavenly Kingdom.

  The word *agios* (or *agia* for female) is the title put in front of a saint's name. For instance, St. Nicholas in Greek is *Agios Nikolaos*, and St. Katherine is *Agia Ekaterini*. Agios/agia can also be translated as "holy." Thus, the name of each saint is Holy Nicholas or Holy Katherine. As we chant this hymn, we pray that the title "holy" is now conferred upon our deceased loved one, that they have taken their place together with all of God's saints. We are also praying that our loved one has earned this title and is considered "holy" by our Lord.

+ **A desire to be holy.** I have mentioned at many funerals that we will all one day be the guest of honor at a funeral—our own. We pray that at that time, God will deem us also worthy of the title "holy," which should be a goal that drives and motivates us. A friend of mine, when talking about our lifespan, once said to me, "We are all guests," meaning that we are all just passing through this life. It is temporary for all of us. A guest in a home is someone who is there one day and not there the next. The owner is the one who stays permanently. None of us will stay here permanently; we are all guests of God in this life. A funeral is a great reminder of that.

+ **A glimpse of heaven.** We will be discussing this further. For now, the hymnographer gives us three descriptions of life in heaven: "no pain, no sorrow, no sighing." In other words, no suffering, no sadness, and no regret. Rather, there is *life* everlasting. Remember that earlier in this book, we defined life as being with God and death as a state of being absent from God. This hymn prays that we will have life with God and have it forever.

The hymns of the Orthodox funeral service give us comfort when thinking about our deceased loved ones and also give us something to aim for in our own lives.

> With my whole heart I cry; answer me, O LORD!
>> I will keep thy statutes.
> I cry to thee; save me,
>> that I may observe thy testimonies.
> I rise before dawn and cry for help;
>> I hope in thy words.
> My eyes are awake before the watches of the night,
>> that I may meditate upon thy promise.
> Hear my voice in thy steadfast love;
>> O LORD, in thy justice preserve my life.
> They draw near who persecute me with evil purpose;
>> they are far from thy law.
> But thou art near, O LORD,
>> and all thy commandments are true.
> Long have I known from thy testimonies
>> that thou hast founded them forever.
> (Psalm 119:145–152)

An Opportunity for Education

Listen to advice and accept instruction,
that you may gain wisdom for the future.

Proverbs 19:20

O nly in recent centuries have people been afforded the opportunity to read. Before the invention of the printing press,
there were very few books and manuscripts, and only a few people
could read them. In composing the great anthology of hymns in our
Church, hymnographers were intentional in writing hymns that not
only praised God and offered supplication to Him; the vast majority
of them are actually hymns that teach. We learn through repetition,
and hearing hymns over and over again is a way for Christians to
learn and understand the Faith.

Impermanence

Saint John of Damascus (675–749) composed most of the funeral
service, including thirteen hymns called *idiomela* that give us not
only an opportunity to grieve but also to reflect and to learn. These
hymns read as a sermon on the subject of death, why it happens,

and why the sacrifice of Christ and His Resurrection are important. Here are a few quotes from these hymns:[39]

> Which of life's pleasures remains free of sorrow? Which earthly glory is permanent? All this is fainter than a shadow, all more illusory than a dream. In a single moment, death succeeds them all. O Christ, grant rest to those whom You have taken, in the light of Your face and in the sweetness of Your handsomeness, O benevolent Lord. (Idiomelon of the first mode)

When I chant this hymn, the initial two questions are very thought provoking. None of life's pleasures remain free of sorrow. That's true. Even the best day has an ending. Thus, death is not unlike sorrows we've experienced in life, except that it is permanent. In contrast, no earthly glory is permanent. People graduate from schools, become too old to play competitive sports, and retire from jobs—three pursuits, among many, that bring "glory" in life. Of course, we know that in a single moment, death can end life and any earthly glory that came along with it. This hymn offers a sober reminder not to put all our focus on earthly glory instead of on the Lord and His eternal glory. Our visions of long life, wealth, and security are just illusions because death can come literally at any moment, and all those things will end.

The Great Equalizer

I remembered how the Prophet once said: "I am but dust and ashes"; and then I looked into the graves and saw the naked bones, and in turn I exclaimed: "Who can tell, which one was a king, which one a soldier, rich or poor, a righteous man or a

---

39 "Sacraments and Blessings: Funeral," 3-5.

sinner?" Nevertheless, O Lord, grant that Your servants may rest with the righteous, in Your benevolence. (Idiomelon of plagal first mode)

Death is the great equalizer. This hymn paints the picture of a prophet looking into many tombs, and he can't tell which bones belonged to a rich man, a king, a soldier, a poor man, a sinner, or a saint, because all the bones look the same. It's ironic that in life, we clamor about equality and fight to get ahead. We fail to realize that one day we will all be *equally* dead. In that sense, every funeral I have served has been the same. All the people laid to rest have been equally dead.

Death Was Not God's Intention

In the beginning, when You fashioned man in Your image and likeness, You put him in Paradise to have dominion over Your creation. But by the envy of the devil, man was deceived; and he ate the fruit and thus became a transgressor of Your commandments. Therefore, O Lord, You sentenced him to return to the earth, from which he had been taken, and to pray for repose. (Idiomelon of the grave mode)

This hymn tells us once again the reason why people die, and that this was not God's intention for us when He created us. It reminds us that we were created in God's image and likeness, and placed in Paradise to have dominion over creation and continuous communion with God. The Fall is our separation from God rather than His separation from us. It came as a result of the devil's envy and humanity being deceived by a lie, and the consequence of this was an earthly death and the need to pray for eternal rest again in Paradise.

Resurrection Hope

The series of hymns comes to its conclusion with a joyful hymn. It speaks of Christ lying in the Tomb for our salvation and opening again the gates to Paradise through His descent into Hades and His Resurrection from the dead. Because He has made Paradise possible, we then pray for the same gift to be given to the one who has passed away.

> O Lord, Your death gave rise to immortality; for if You had not been enclosed in a tomb, then Paradise would not have been opened. Therefore grant repose to the departed, O benevolent God. (Idiomelon of plagal fourth mode)

The Church, in her wisdom, has created a service to allow us both to grieve and to learn. The hymns touch our hearts as they give us an opportunity to mourn the loss of a loved one. They touch our minds as they allow us to think about death. And they touch our souls as they ask us to reflect on our own death.

We will go to many funerals in our lives and will experience many opportunities to learn about life and death. When we were in school and we knew a test was coming, we studied and prepared. Even though we might have been nervous on the day of the test, the fact of the upcoming test and the questions on it were not a total surprise.

It's the same way with life and death. "Studying" the hymns at a funeral service gives us familiarity with death so that when it comes, it is not a surprise, and we are more prepared because we've studied. Of course, study without application is not useful. Thus, it is important that we apply what we learn. However, it is also critical that as we are going about living our lives, we remember our eventual destination before God's seat of judgment so that we add a "why" to the "what" that we are doing. The funeral service is a big help in bringing this to mind.

> Look on my affliction and deliver me,
>   for I do not forget thy law.
> Please my cause and redeem me;
>   give me life according to thy promise!
> Salvation is far from the wicked,
>   for they do not seek thy statutes.
> Great is thy mercy, O LORD;
>   give me life according to thy justice.
> Many are my persecutors and my adversaries,
>   but I do not swerve from thy testimonies.
> I look at the faithless with disgust,
>   because they do not keep thy commands.
> Consider how I love thy precepts!
>   Preserve my life according to thy steadfast love.
> The sum of thy word is truth;
>   and everyone of thy righteous ordinances endures for ever.
> (Psalm 119:153–160)

Blessed Is the Way

Jesus said to her, "I am the resurrection and the life; he who believes in me, though he die, yet shall he live, and whoever lives and believes in me shall never die."

John 11:25–26

In contemporary times, "celebrations of life" are replacing traditional funeral services. Many people think that funeral services, especially the way the Orthodox service is done with an open casket, are kind of morbid. Having been Orthodox my whole life and having served as a priest for many years, I'm not only used to our funeral service, but I have come to appreciate its nuances. I grant you that a funeral chanted all in Greek with a chanter who rushes through the service as if he's got somewhere else to go is not very inspiring, and I've experienced a few of these.[40] When offered properly, with purposeful singing and thoughtful remarks by the priest, the funeral becomes not only a time for reflection and grief, but the hymns are also soothing to the soul, especially the hymn we are reflecting on in this section.

As we discussed in the previous reflection, in the funeral service we begin with a plea to God for mercy then sing several hymns of

---

40 I'm thankful that this hasn't happened in my own parish, where our chanters have always been conscientious and sensitive at funerals.

education. Next, the tone of the funeral turns to blessings for the deceased and comfort for those who are left behind. After the idiomela hymns, which are primarily educational, we sing a hymn called the *prokeimenon*: "Blessed ever be the way, the way on which you walk this day, for there is prepared for you a place of everlasting rest."[41] Unfortunately, I can't sing this hymn for you through writing, but if you ever hear it sung well, you will experience a short but magnificent composition. The arrangement that our choir sings at funerals is calming, and people can almost get lost in this hymn and feel not only a temporary reprieve from sorrow, but as if they were on the road to Paradise.

Of course, it is important to "celebrate" the life of the deceased. Photo collections, stories, memories, inside jokes—these are things that continually bring to our minds why someone was important in our lives. There is nothing wrong with remembering people and celebrating them. The funeral service serves as a celebration of eternal life, the fact that there is life after death, and the hope that our loved one will participate eternally in God's glory. Indeed, when we have confidence in this hope, we can truthfully sing that the way on which the deceased is walking on the day of their funeral is blessed.

I Am the Resurrection

In Exodus 3, we read the story of Moses encountering a burning bush. God speaks to Moses out of the bush and tells him that he should go tell Pharaoh to let the children of Israel go after their years of enslavement in Egypt. Moses asks God,

> "If I come to the people of Israel and say to them, 'The God of your fathers has sent me to you,' and they ask me, 'What is

---

41   Kezios, *Servants and Sacraments*, Book Three, 21.

his name?' what shall I say to them?" God said to Moses, "I AM WHO I AM." And he said, "Say this to the people of Israel, 'I AM has sent me to you.'" (Ex. 3:13–14)

In Hebrew the name of God is *Yahweh*, and in English, it is simply "I AM." Jesus reveals Himself as God by using "I AM" several times in the Gospel of John.

The verse that precedes this reflection comes from the Gospel account of the raising of Lazarus. We've already discussed how sad Jesus was that His friend had died. Mary, her sister Martha, and their brother Lazarus were friends of Jesus. He would stop by their home often. So this visit was undoubtedly sad and perhaps even a tad uncomfortable. It is very possible that Mary and Martha were disappointed that their miracle-working friend, Jesus, did not stop Lazarus from dying. In John 11:21–27, Martha even says this to Jesus: "Lord, if you had been here, my brother would not have died. And even now I know that whatever you ask from God, God will give you." Indeed, Martha shows faith when she calls Jesus "Lord," and she shows confidence when she says that "even now" something good can happen.

Jesus comforts her with the words, "Your brother will rise again."

Martha answers, "I know that he will rise again in the resurrection at the last day."

And then Jesus changes the entire tenor of the conversation when He says to Martha, "I am the resurrection and the life; he who believes in me, though he die, yet shall he live, and whoever lives and believes in me shall never die." Jesus tells her that the resurrection is not just a far-off hope; He *is* the Resurrection and the life, and those who live and believe (both are necessary) in Jesus will never die—they will never be separated from the love of God, even in physical death.

Jesus then asks Martha, "Do you believe this?" And Martha, previously chastised for being "anxious and troubled about many things"

(Luke 10:41), not only makes a confession of faith but does so in a great act of courage, in the presence of so many Jewish authorities who were hostile to Jesus. She says, "Yes, Lord; I believe that you are the Christ, the Son of God, he who is coming into the world."

Blessed Ever Be the Way

The tenor of the funeral service changes with the hymn, "Blessed Ever Be the Way." Up to this point, we've been praying for God to have pity and be merciful, to forgive and extend grace. We've learned a lot about death, dying, and forgiveness through the hymns. Now this hymn seems to rise above the others in a tone of empowerment, of joy, even of exaltation.

When Martha was speaking to Jesus, Lazarus was still dead. In fact, after this conversation Jesus wept. Imagine, however, that for a moment both forget their grief as Jesus says that He is the Resurrection and Martha confesses Jesus to be the Christ. Indeed, that conversation was blessed, just as the path on which the deceased person passes is blessed: Now they have the opportunity to be empowered with joy greater than any joy they have felt on earth. It is normal to grieve the loss of a loved one. However, as Christians who believe in eternal life, the passing of the beloved should also evoke feelings of joy that they have entered into everlasting rest with the Lord.

While many fear the path of death, the Church speaks of that way as a blessed one. It leads to everlasting rest in the Kingdom of heaven.

> Princes persecute me without cause,
>   but my heart stands in awe of thy words.
> I rejoice at thy word
>   like one who finds great spoil.
> I hate and abhor falsehood,
>   but I love thy law.

Seven times a day I praise thee
    for thy righteous ordinances.
Great peace have those who love thy law;
    nothing can make them stumble.
I hope for thy salvation, O Lord,
    and I do thy commandments.
My soul keeps thy testimonies;
    I love them exceedingly.
I keep thy precepts and testimonies,
    for all my ways are before thee.
(Psalm 119:161–168)

Don't Grieve Like the Others

But we would not have you ignorant, brethren, concerning those who are asleep, that you may not grieve as others do who have no hope. For since we believe that Jesus died and rose again, even so, through Jesus, God will bring with him those who have fallen asleep.

1 Thessalonians 4:13–14

The epistle lesson at the funeral service is from St. Paul's First Letter to the Thessalonians, chapter four, verses 13–17. The passage begins by saying, "We would not have you ignorant, brethren, concerning those who are asleep, that you may not grieve as others do who have no hope." It is important to know that the passage does not say "do not grieve" but rather to "not grieve as others do."

Jesus Grieved

There are two instances in the Bible where Jesus grieved. One was for His friend Lazarus, who had died. Jesus went to the tomb and wept there. Even the Son of God was crying for a friend who had passed. If Jesus can cry, it is okay for us to cry. There are lots of people who think that tears are a sign of weakness, that one must be stoic at all times. But tears express the emotion of grief—and sometimes of joy.

Just as our life would feel incomplete if we never laughed, so it would also feel incomplete if we never cried. It is important that tears come when someone dies. When my dad passed away, I cried on the airplane all the way from Florida to California. Yet I didn't cry at his funeral. That was not because I'm stoic or unfeeling. I have cried for many people that I have buried; I just generally do not cry in public. God brings the tears at other times so that when I'm presiding at a funeral, I can lead the worship without being emotional. I cry often, actually.

The second time that we read of Jesus crying is in the Garden of Gethsemane, shortly before He was arrested and crucified. Jesus cried these tears in anticipation of His own death. He was scared not only at the prospect of dying but of how He was going to die. He knew that pain and suffering stood between Him and death. Again, using Jesus as the example, it is okay to cry as we reflect on our own death. If one is facing major surgery in order to extend life (a multiple bypass, for example), it is certainly okay to grieve, to cry, to express emotion. No need to be stoic in this instance either.

Healthy and Chaotic Grief

There is a difference, I believe, in healthy grieving and chaotic grieving. I've been to funerals where people were wailing in the pews, where people have tried to climb into the casket, and where someone actually jumped down into the grave. I think that is the "ignorant" behavior that St. Paul refers to in his Epistle to the Thessalonians. Because we believe in God, because we believe in the mercy of God, and because we believe in the Kingdom of God, we can have human sadness and cry and grieve, but we shouldn't feel chaotic, as if all hope is gone. As Christians, we know we have hope. Saint Paul confirms in the very next verse, "For since we believe that Jesus died and rose again, even so, through Jesus, God will bring with Him those who have fallen asleep."

I have experienced many deaths that I would describe as horrific: accidents, murder—yes, we had a double murder of a mother and her daughter-in-law in our community several years ago—and several deaths of children. A great emotional outpouring occurred at many of these funerals, loud questions as to why this happened. That is to be expected. However, with time and space, even in such terrible deaths we can step back from grief and take some measure of comfort in these words of St. Paul. Those who have passed on will rise again to a better life, made possible through the death and Resurrection of Christ and the mercies of God.

Saint Paul concludes this short passage with the comforting words, "we shall always be with the Lord." The choice to believe in God is just that: a choice. There are many ignorant voices in the world who claim that Christians are the problem and that Christ is a construct to give people something to lean on when life gets tough. Those thoughts are personal choices. I choose to believe in God, even though in many ways I'm still ignorant of many things.

I remember the first time my wife and I saw a sonogram of our son in her womb, of this little baby growing inside her. I was fascinated and thought to myself, "This confirms the presence of God to me." How could life possibly be authored by us? Perhaps it is continued by us, but it was authored by Him. On the other end of life, I have seen so many beautiful things that have happened surrounding the passing of people. These experiences confirm for me the reality of God even though, again, I'm still ignorant of so much.

I have grieved the loss of many people—my parents, parishioners, friends—but I do it with a measure of spiritual hope mixed with my human sadness. And hope is something that eventually should trump sadness and despair. We grieve, but we do so with hope.

I will bless the Lord at all times;
    his praise shall continually be in my mouth.
My soul makes its boast in the Lord;
    let the afflicted hear and be glad.
O magnify the Lord with me,
    and let us exult his name together!

I sought the Lord and he answered me,
    and delivered me from all my fears.
Look to him, and be radiant;
    so your faces shall never be ashamed.
This poor man cried, and the Lord heard him,
    and saved him out of all his troubles.
The angel of the Lord encamps
    around those who fear him, and delivers them.
O taste and see that the Lord is good!
    Happy is the man who takes refuge in him!
O fear the Lord, you his saints,
    for those who fear him have no want!
The young lions suffer want and hunger;
    but those who seek the Lord lack no good thing.

Come, O sons, listen to me,
    I will teach you the fear of the Lord.
What man is there who desires life,
    and covets many days, that he may enjoy good?
Keep your tongue from evil,
    and your lips from speaking deceit.
Depart from evil, and do good;
    seek peace, and pursue it.

The eyes of the Lord are toward the righteous,
    and his ears toward their cry.
The face of the Lord is against evildoers,
    to cut off the remembrance of them from the earth.
When the righteous cry for help, the Lord hears,
    and delivers them out of all their troubles.
The Lord is near to the brokenhearted,
    and saves the crushed in spirit.

Many are the afflictions of the righteous;
    but the Lord delivers him out of them all.
He keeps all his bones;
    not one of them is broken.
Evil shall slay the wicked;
    and those who hate the righteous will be condemned.
The Lord redeems the life of his servants;
    none of those who take refuge in him will be condemned.
(Psalm 34)

Those Who Have Done Good

Do not marvel at this; for the hour is coming when all who
are in the tombs will hear his voice and come forth, those who
have done good, to the resurrection of life, and those who have
done evil, to the resurrection of judgment.

John 5:28–29

The Gospel lesson at a funeral service comes from John 5:24–30.
While the passage ostensibly speaks about the authority of the
Son of God in relation to God the Father, it also contains specific
teaching on death. It begins with Jesus' words: "Truly, truly I say to
you, he who hears my word and believes him who sent me has eternal
life; he does not come into judgment, but has passed from death to
life." If *life* refers to being in the presence of God, and *death* is being
absent from God, then we see that *judgment* (or condemnation) is
used synonymously with *death* in this passage. Thus, those who
believe in Jesus as the Son of God do not come into judgment but
pass from death and enter eternal life.

We also know that it is not only belief that leads to salvation.
There must be work, and there is also the grace of God that allows
us to enter into eternal life. In 5:29, we read the word *done* two
times, confirming it is not only what we believe but what we "do"
with that. Jesus says that "those who have done good" will go to the

"resurrection of life," and "those who have done evil" will go "to the resurrection of judgment."

Authoritative and Non-Authoritative Teachings

This brings us to the question, What exactly happens when we die? There are a lot of teachings out there about this from both Orthodox and non-Orthodox sources that use terms like "toll houses" and "trials." Some speak of purgatory, a Catholic doctrine that teaches that a person enters a state where they must undergo purification from their sins.[42] The Orthodox Church rejects the idea of purgatory because it is not found in the Scriptures or in the writings of the Fathers.

Let us introduce another term used both by the Orthodox and the Roman Catholics: *theologoumenon*. It means, for the Orthodox, a "theological statement or concept in the area of individual opinion rather than of authoritative doctrine."[43] It can be defined further as an orthodox theological opinion that over time becomes pious tradition even if it is erroneous or imperfect. A lot of beliefs about death and what happens afterward can be categorized as theologoumenon.

A theologoumenon is based on Scripture, which leads to some logical conclusions. For instance, in Matthew 22:30, concerning marriage in heaven, Jesus says, "For in the resurrection they neither marry nor are given in marriage, but are like angels in heaven." From this statement, we can deduce not only that there is not a

---

42 This teaching is based in part on Revelation 21:27, where we read, "Nothing unclean shall enter it, nor any one who practices abomination or falsehood, but only those who are written in the Lamb's book of life." See https://www.catholic.com/qa/what-is-purgatory.

43 *Merriam-Webster's Unabridged Dictionary*, Merriam-Webster, https://unabridged.merriam-webster.com/unabridged/theologoumenon. Accessed Aug. 14, 2025.

classification of married or unmarried in heaven, but that other classifications, such as rich or poor, educated or uneducated, with children or without children, would not exist in heaven as well. We don't *know* this, because we haven't been to heaven and come back to talk about it, but we can deduce things like this from Scripture.

God's Basis for Judgment

Many places in the Bible give insight into a judgment that will happen before God. We've discussed already the Parable of the Talents, where the servants were entrusted with talents and "after a long time the master of those servants came and settled accounts with them" (Matt. 25:19). In the parable, the master is God, who entrusts talents (time, ability, opportunity) to each person, and at some point we will have to give an account to Him for what we did with the gifts He gave us. Even more succinct is Matthew 25:31–46, where we read about the judgment of the nations, when everyone will be gathered before the throne of God. This judgment will be based on six standards: "I was hungry and you gave me food; I was thirsty and you gave me drink; I was a stranger and you welcomed me; I was naked and you clothed me; I was sick and you visited me; I was in prison and you came to me" (vv. 35–36).

We all have regrets about things we didn't do or should have done. There are sins of commission, where we actively do something wrong, like hit another person—we are committing a wrong. There are also sins of omission, which is failure to do something we should have done, such as seeing someone who is wounded and passing by on the other side, as we read in the Parable of the Good Samaritan (Luke 10:25–37). The priest and Levite did not cause the misfortune of the man who was robbed and left for dead, but in not ministering to him, they committed a sin of indifference, or omission. They failed to love their neighbor.

When Will the Judgment Occur?

Another question is exactly when we will go to heaven and when will the judgment be. In Luke 23:43, Jesus tells the thief on the cross, "Today you will be with me in Paradise," which seems to indicate that we go to heaven, if that is our destination, immediately after death. But Matthew 25:31–33 seems to be in direct contradiction to this when Jesus says, "When the Son of Man comes in his glory, and all the angels with him, then he will sit on his glorious throne. Before him will be gathered all the nations, and he will separate them one from another as a shepherd separates the sheep from the goats, and he will place the sheep at his right hand, but the goats at the left." This seems to indicate that the judgment will take place at the end of time, and that we won't enter Paradise until then.

Then there is 2 Peter 3:8, which reads, "But do not ignore this one fact, beloved, that with the Lord one day is as a thousand years, and a thousand years as one day." This seems to indicate that our time and God's time work in different ways, on different planes. Does this then leave open the possibility that on the day a person passes away they enter God's time and that the day they die and the day of the Last Judgment actually can be the same day? This verse seems to leave the door to this possibility open.

The Orthodox Church teaches about individual judgment as well as the Last Judgment later at the general resurrection. Scripture supports both concepts. Ultimately, how the judgment will work is the purview of God, so even as we try to understand or conjecture what may happen, we cannot fully comprehend how the judgment will work.

It is very dangerous to try to speak dogmatically about this subject. There are certainly much more educated theologians and God-inspired saints than me out there—I am neither. What I believe is what the Church teaches: I will stand in judgment one day before the Lord and give account for the things I did with my life. And then

God will judge whether I am worthy to enter into Paradise or not. I believe that with certainty!

The Certainty of Judgment

Not every person will be judged worthy to enter into everlasting life. That's why Jesus indicates there is a judgment, not just an automatic entrance into the Kingdom of God. Therefore, what we believe, and what we do with our belief, absolutely matter. In our world of political correctness, people think that God wouldn't dare discriminate against anyone and not allow them into heaven. The Bible does not support this.

Matthew 24:40–41 reads, "Then two men will be in the field; one is taken and one is left. Two women will be grinding at the mill; one is taken and one is left." A cursory reading seems to indicate that fifty percent will go to heaven and fifty percent do not. This idea then causes people to judge themselves against others: "If I'm in the top fifty percent, I'm in!" But percentages are irrelevant. Jesus says in the Bible, confirmed in the reading from the Gospel of John at the funeral, that some will go to the resurrection of life and some will go to the resurrection of judgment, or condemnation. The Parable of the Rich Man and Lazarus (Luke 16:19–31) also supports that not everyone will go to heaven. Other theories, like the coming of a "rapture" when Jesus will return to take Christians to heaven during the end times, have a lot of traction in some churches. But this teaching is only about two hundred years old and is not an Orthodox doctrine.

What the Church teaches with certainty is that there is a judgment for all of us that determines our eternal destiny in heaven or in hell. I don't know when that judgment will be, and I don't know how much longer I will live. Therefore, my main concern is my stewardship of today—what I am doing with this day that God has given to me.

The decision on how we live our lives today goes back to how we view salvation. I have the potential to be saved because of the death and Resurrection of Christ and my entrance into the life of Christ through the Sacrament of Baptism. I am working on my salvation based on how I glorify God and serve others today. I will (hopefully) be saved by His grace, which will be extended (or not) at my judgment before His throne. This is why we pray for His grace, believe in it, and ultimately must trust in it. This is another example of what faith is—not only to believe in God, but to trust in the mercy and grace of God.

I personally don't get wrapped up in the details. I focus on giving God glory through serving others today. The judgment is His and His alone. I will fare better at the judgment if I've been faithful with what He has entrusted me.

Hear this, all peoples!
Give ear, all inhabitants of the world,
both low and high,
    rich and poor together!
My mouth shall speak wisdom;
    the meditation of my heart shall be understanding.
I will incline my ear to a proverb;
    I will solve my riddle to the music of the lyre.

Why should I fear in times of trouble,
    when the iniquity of my persecutors surrounds me,
men who trust in their wealth
    and boast of the abundance of their riches?
Truly no man can ransom himself,
    or give to God the price of his life,
for the ransom of his life is costly,
    and can never suffice,

that he should continue to live on for ever,
    and never see the Pit.

Yea, he shall see that even the wise die,
    the fool and the stupid alike
      must perish and leave their wealth to others.
Their graves are their homes for ever,
    their dwelling places to all generations,
      though they named lands their own.
Man cannot abide in his pomp,
    he is like the beasts that perish.
This is the fate of those who have foolish confidence,
    the end of those who are pleased with their portion.
Like sheep they are appointed for Sheol;
    Death shall be their shepherd;
straight to the grave they descend,
    and their form shall waste away;
      Sheol shall be their home.
But God will ransom my soul from the power of Sheol,
    for he will receive me.

Be not afraid when one becomes rich,
    when the glory of his house increases.
For when he dies he will carry nothing away;
    his glory will not go down after him.
Though, while he lives, he counts himself happy,
    and though a man gets praise when he does well for himself,
he will go to the generation of his fathers,
    who will never more see the light.
Man cannot abide in his pomp,
    he is like the beasts that perish.
(Psalm 49)

Memory Eternal

For the righteous will never be moved;
he will be remembered for ever.

Psalm 112:6

As the funeral comes to an end, we sing a simple yet beautiful and powerful hymn, "Memory Eternal." This hymn evokes emotion; it is probably the most emotional hymn in the funeral. It's the hymn that confirms that our loved one is now a memory, not someone with whom we will sit at the dinner table, or laugh, or spend the holidays. When someone who is grieving is able to pause for a moment in the shock and extreme sorrow that often follow a death, this hymn can be one of inspiration, that the memory of someone will live on.

It is also a plea to God to remember our loved one in His Kingdom, forever. When more than one clergyman is present at an Orthodox Liturgy, there are multiple occasions when the clergy will turn to each other and say, "May the Lord our God remember your (archpriesthood, priesthood, or diaconate) in His Kingdom, now and forever and to the ages of ages. Amen."[44] This is a prayer and plea to God for remembrance and, by extension, grace and

---

44   This occurs at the beginning of the Divine Liturgy, after the Great Entrance, and when the clergy ask forgiveness before receiving Holy Communion.

mercy—in this case on fellow clergymen who are alive. The same principle applies to those who have passed; the remaining loved ones sing "memory eternal" with the prayer that God will remember them in His heavenly Kingdom.

Someone once said at a funeral, "When someone dies, part of you dies with them. However, part of them lives in you." People have come and gone throughout my life, but pieces of them live on in me, and they add a depth to who I am. It's like people who collect passport stamps of all the places they've been to, or people like me who are trying to visit all fifty of the United States (forty-seven as of this writing). I may have been a resident of Florida for the past twenty years, but pieces of beauty from each state I've visited create depth in my life experience. As I go through life, I collect memories, inspiration, and life lessons from the people whose paths have crossed mine.

Their Influence Lives On in Us

I met a man named John many years ago, and the first time I shook his hand, he said my grip should be stronger. He would shake a hand almost hard enough to break it. I think of John often when I shake hands with someone.

Father John was one of my priests when I was between nine and fourteen years old—some very impressionable years. I loved how he celebrated the Divine Liturgy. Some of his gestures definitely live on in my liturgical mannerisms.

Innumerable people have left impressions on my life and given me good quotes, mottos, and advice. Many of these people, thankfully, are still alive. When they pass away, their advice and lessons will continue to shape my life, and I will remember them.

Over the years, several people have offered me gifts that I have used to buy my priestly vestments. I can remember the year I bought each set and the ones who offered me the gifts that enabled me to purchase them.

Think of the people who have influenced you, especially the ones who have passed on. While you may miss them, even a lot, pause to be thankful that their path crossed yours and that their memory lives on in your life.

Uniting the Church in Heaven and on Earth

We've already discussed the concept of the Church Militant and the Church Triumphant. The Orthodox Church has two very specific liturgical acts that unite the two, connecting those who have passed away with those who are still living on earth.

The stole of the priest traditionally has two rows of fringe at the bottom. One represents the Church Militant, and one represents the Church Triumphant. Each time the priest puts on his stole for something as big as a packed church on Pascha or a wedding, or something small like a confession or a hospital visit, he does so while bringing with him the whole Church. The entire Church, symbolized on the stole, gathers for each service, each sacrament, each house blessing, each time the priest puts on his stole and exercises his priestly function.

The second liturgical act that connects the two is the preparation and consecration of the Holy Gifts. In the Proskomide, the service of preparation of the Holy Gifts, the priest takes crumbs of bread and places them on the diskos, or paten, for those belonging to the Church Militant and those belonging to the Church Triumphant. He prays for people by name in both categories. Both my parents are deceased, and my brother and his family live in California. In the preparation of the Holy Gifts before each Divine Liturgy, I pray for my family and for my brother's family and place particles of bread on the left side of the diskos, which is reserved for the Church Militant.

I then remember my parents and place particles for them on the right side of the diskos, which is reserved for the Church Triumphant.

Even though I will never share a dinner table with my parents again and I rarely do with my brother, our whole family is together on the holy altar table each time I celebrate the Divine Liturgy. This is the place we can always be with our loved ones. When you want to remember someone, just give their name to your priest and ask him to commemorate them when he prepares the Holy Gifts.

At the time of the consecration of the Holy Gifts, when we kneel and pray for the Holy Spirit to descend on the bread and wine and consecrate them into the Body and Blood of Christ, the priest elevates the Gifts with these words: "Your own of Your own we offer to You, in all and for all."[45] "For all" is a true statement, as it covers those who are in the Church Militant and those who are in the Church Triumphant. After the Holy Gifts have been consecrated, the priest prays, "Again, we offer You this spiritual worship for those who have reposed in the faith: forefathers, fathers, patriarchs, prophets, apostles, preachers, evangelists, martyrs, confessors, ascetics, and for every righteous spirit made perfect in faith."[46] That covers all those who have come before us and connects us with them at the most solemn moment of every Divine Liturgy.

Memorials as the Years Go By

We also remember our loved ones liturgically at memorial services that are held at various intervals after a person has passed away. Commonly a memorial service is conducted after forty days—the interval of time between the Resurrection and the Ascension of Christ—and on the yearly anniversary of the death. In parts of the world where it

---

45 *The Divine Liturgy of St. John Chrysostom* (2015), 53.
46 *Divine Liturgy* (2015), 55.

is customary to disinter remains, such as in Greece (where they do not typically embalm people), this disinterment is done after three years, and the remains are consolidated into a smaller container and reinterred. This is the reason for the three-year memorial. Since disinterment is not done in the United States, there is no "need" for a three-year memorial, although they are common.

Memorials are also offered each year on four Saturdays known as "Saturday of the Souls." Three are at the beginning of Lent, and one is the Saturday before Pentecost. Memorials are not done on feast days of the Lord and the Virgin Mary, nor from the Saturday of Lazarus through Thomas Sunday. The tradition of offering koliva, or boiled wheat, at a memorial service comes from John 12:24, where Jesus says to His disciples, "Truly, truly, I say to you, unless a grain of wheat falls into the earth and dies, it remains alone; but if it dies, it bears much fruit." The most basic food of humanity is bread. Bread comes from wheat, and wheat comes from seeds that are separated from the stalk (and essentially are dead), which are then planted into the earth and come alive again as a stalk of wheat. In the same way, we die and enter into the earth but rise to a much greater life.

Oil and Earth

There is nothing wrong with going to a cemetery to "visit" our loved ones. It gives us a tangible place to go and feel connected to them. However, the best place to feel connected is actually in the Divine Liturgy. Every Divine Liturgy includes a petition: "And remember those whom each one of us has in mind, and all the people."[47] This prayer, along with others, continually offers us an opportunity to bring anyone to mind.

---

47 *The Divine Liturgy of St. John Chrysostom* (2015), 59.

As we discussed earlier, the funeral service concludes with the priest placing oil and earth on the deceased. This used to be done in cemeteries, but because most municipalities prohibit opening the casket there, it is done generally in the church.[48] As the priest places the oil over the deceased, he prays a verse from Psalm 51: "Purge me with hyssop, and I shall be clean; wash me and I shall be whiter than snow" (v. 7). When he places the earth over the deceased, he says the words from Genesis 3 that God spoke to Adam and Eve, giving them the final consequence of the Fall: "You are dust, and to dust you shall return" (v. 19).

The people in attendance should greet each other with the words, "May his/her memory be eternal." There is a Greek custom where people say "*Zoi se mas*," which literally is translated "Life to us." This is a good or bad phrase, depending on how one means it. If "life" is referring to life on earth, then this is a bad phrase. It's like saying "Life to us who are living. Thankfully we are not the one who has passed." But if "life" is referring to eternal life, then it is a good phrase, because it means we hope for eternal life for ourselves who are left, just as we hope it for the person who has passed.

The better phrase to say when someone has passed is "Memory eternal," or "May his/her memory be eternal." This means that the life of the deceased is worthy to be remembered and that each of us will carry something of them with us as we continue on. It is also a prayer that they may be remembered by God and thus live eternally.

May the memory of our loved ones be eternal, and may God grant us comfort as we grieve, joy as we remember, and strength as we go on.

---

48 Some Orthodox jurisdictions place oil and earth on top of a closed casket during the graveside service at the cemetery, before it is lowered into the ground, or in some cases after it has been lowered into the ground. The Greek Orthodox Church places oil and earth on the body of the deceased in the church before the casket is closed for the final time.

Let my cry come before thee, O LORD;
   give me understanding according to thy word!
Let my supplication come before thee;
   deliver me according to thy word.
My lips will pour forth praise
   that thou dost teach me thy statutes.
My tongue will sing of thy word,
   for all thy commandments are right.
Let thy hand be ready to help me,
   for I have chosen thy precepts.
I long for thy salvation, O LORD,
   and thy law is my delight.
Let me live, that I may praise thee,
   and let thy ordinances help me.
I have gone astray like a lost sheep; seek thy servant,
   for I do not forget thy commandments.
(Psalm 119:169–176)

Heaven and the Good Lord—Fr. Constantine

I believe that I shall see the goodness of the LORD
   in the land of the living!
Wait for the LORD;
   be strong, and let your heart take courage;
yea, wait for the LORD!

Psalm 27:13–14

I've known Fr. Constantine for over thirty years. When I first went to the seminary back in 1994, he was the priest at a local parish in Boston. When I was a deacon, I served with him in his parish many times. He is retired in Florida now, and our paths cross at least once a year. We make it a point to chat on the phone at least once a month. Father Constantine is thirty-five years older than I, and he has been a priest longer than I have been alive. He is the closest man to a father figure I still have left. I treasure our relationship.

For most of his life, Fr. Constantine was married to Presbytera Helen. They enjoyed marriage, raising children, and ministry. In their later years, retired from full-time ministry (though still serving into his late 80s), Fr. Constantine devoted himself to caring for Presbytera Helen, who battled various health ailments. He never complained about it; neither did she complain about her challenges.

Father Constantine also has been slowed down by various maladies and never complains about them.

Every person we meet has the potential to touch our lives in a memorable way. Father Constantine is a superb liturgist, an amazing chanter, a thoughtful speaker, and a compassionate pastor. But these are not the reasons I admire him. No, there are three words that he says frequently—"The good Lord"—and these are the words I will remember him by. Because no matter what happens in his life, he always refers to the goodness of the Lord.

Shortly before Presbytera Helen passed away, he said to me, "I think the good Lord is ready to take Presbytera. I am not ready to let her go, but if this is what the good Lord wants, then I have to find a way to be okay with that." Father Constantine is not of my generation; he was born in Greece, so he is not even native to our country. While much of the world, especially the younger generation, either does not believe in God or, worse yet, curses the will of God, Fr. Constantine rejoices in the Lord in good times and bad times.

When I found out that Presbytera Helen had passed away, I called Fr. Constantine to express my condolences. The first thing he said to me was, "The good Lord came for Presbytera last night."

Experiencing the Goodness of God

If we truly believe in God, if we truly believe in His goodness, then not only will we speak about His goodness, we also will live out that goodness, we will desire that goodness, and we will anticipate the fullness of that goodness when we prepare to depart this life.

I see colorful advertisements for exotic places I'd love to visit all the time on the computer. Color photos, videos, and testimonials get us excited about going to places we've never been. Part of the challenge of Christianity is that we don't have photos, videos, or testimonials of our desired destination, heaven.

We have testimonials from people like Fr. Constantine and the other people I have written about in this book who have lived a life of faith and were faithful at the time of their passing. We have images of holiness, like the icons on the walls of our churches. We have conceptual images, like the song "I Can Only Imagine" by the Christian band *Mercy Me*. We have images of perfection like sunrises and sunsets. Ultimately, to believe in God, to believe that redemption is found in the salvific work of Jesus Christ, and to believe that there is life after death are indeed choices. This is what faith is—a choice to believe in what we do not fully comprehend and what we have not fully seen. I have seen faith in the real-life testimonies of people featured in this book. I have experienced the majesty of God through many of these experiences, even in the ones where someone I loved passed away.

When we were young, many of us were introduced first to the goodness of God. Before we were old enough to read, to study, and to learn complex concepts, we were introduced to the goodness of God. Parents gently point and say, "Look at *Christouli* (Christ)" in an icon. We memorize a simple prayer: "God is great, God is good." This was our introduction to God. We weren't introduced to a scary God or a vengeful God, but a good God. Thus, the common denominator throughout life, even as it gets complicated, even as faith gets challenged by circumstance, even as doubt creeps in, must be remembering the goodness of God, seeing Him as "the good Lord."

The Divine services of our church pray to God as a "good and merciful God." God is described as *philanthropos*, or "friend of man." The world is twisting God into either a politically correct God who accepts all kinds of behavior or into a politically incorrect God who is intolerant and needs to be cancelled. God lives on neither of these extremes.

Like Fr. Constantine, I choose to believe in the goodness of God. Even when life doesn't go as I had hoped, even when I feel disappointed in God—and I do sometimes—I still show up because I believe in Him and in His goodness. In being privileged to see so many people at the end of life, I have seen that those who have faith have such a great peace. This is not a peace of "resignation," as in being resigned to their demise and making peace with their death, but a peace of "conviction": They believe in God, in the goodness of God, and in the mercy that God will have toward them.

If you are reading this message and you haven't begun your journey of faith, if you've begun and taken a detour, or if you began and you have quit, the best place to begin or to restart is by reflecting on the goodness of God. Surround yourself with people who speak of the goodness of God, read the Bible and learn about His goodness, worship in church and reflect on the beauty of His image in the icons, and look to see goodness in others.

We long to experience what others have experienced. For example, I hope before my life is over to visit Iceland. The northern lights, thermal springs, gushing waterfalls, glaciers—I hope to one day see these things. Why? Because people who have visited Iceland have told me about it, because of things I have read, and mostly because of photos that show a place of majesty and beauty. What I've seen and what I've heard makes Iceland seem like a good place to visit. It's the same with God and experiencing His goodness. As Christians, we also have to be ambassadors for the goodness of God; we are to reflect His goodness, and we can talk about His goodness. What a blessing to hear someone, even in sorrow, still be able to talk about "the good Lord."

What will heaven be like? I can only imagine. However, I know what goodness looks like. I even know what the goodness of God looks like. So, I imagine that heaven will be like experiencing an infinite and nonstop, undistracted amount of the goodness of God. And this is what gives me motivation to push through the sorrows and setbacks of life.

If we believe not only in God, but in the goodness of the Lord, what heaven will look like is not important. What is important is that we will be embraced by the eternal and infinite goodness of the Lord. That's all that really matters.

I will pay my vows to the LORD
   in the presence of all his people.
Precious in the sight of the LORD
   is the death of his saints.
O LORD, I am thy servant;
   I am thy servant, the son of thy handmaid.
   Thou hast loosed my bonds.
I will offer to thee the sacrifice of thanksgiving
   and call on the name of the LORD.
I will pay my vows to the LORD
   in the presence of all his people,
in the courts of the house of the LORD,
   in your midst, O Jerusalem.
Praise the LORD!
(Psalm 116:14–19)

Conclusion:
And to Those in the Tombs He Has Granted Life

Surely goodness and mercy shall follow me
all the days of my life;
and I shall dwell in the house of the LORD
for ever.

Psalm 23:6

He has risen, he is not here.

Mark 16:6

I am writing this reflection on my fifty-second birthday. Fifty-three years ago, on March 14, 1971, the Sunday of the Holy Cross, my parents offered a prayer, asking God for a son. (They had been unable to have children.) They promised to name him Stavros ("cross" in English) in honor of the Holy Cross and to give him back to the Church as a priest.

I was born one year later—same date, same hour as they made their prayer. I always knew the story of how I got my name, but I didn't know about their promise to give me to the Church until the day I told them I felt God was calling me to the priesthood. They never told me about the promise, they said, because they didn't want me to feel pressured to become a priest. Instead, they wanted me to discern my calling on my own.

I was ordained a priest in 1998, and despite having served now for nearly twenty-six years, I still have questions, sometimes I still have doubts, and most definitely I make mistakes just like everyone else. The prospect of death doesn't frighten me as much as the prospect of dying, pain, needles, and loss of control. I know that the older I get, the closer I get to these possibilities and this eventuality of dying. There is definitely more life in my rearview mirror than over my horizon.

If there really is nothing after death, then each birthday should be a cause of sadness—one year closer to nothing. However, because I believe in God, in His goodness, and in the salvation made possible through Jesus Christ, each birthday brings me one year closer to entering the Kingdom of God. It also brings me one year closer to my judgment before Him.

The Icon of the Resurrection

The Orthodox icon of the Resurrection does not depict Jesus coming out of the Tomb like Superman, having cheated death. It depicts Him descending into Hades and encountering the souls of all those who died before this time. Adam and Eve are there. Righteous people like John the Baptist and Moses are there. Even people like David, who committed pretty egregious sins, are there. All have a chance to be resurrected because of the Resurrection of Christ.

The miracle of the Resurrection is not just that Jesus rose from the dead, but that because He rose from the dead, He opened the gateway for the rest of us to rise as well.

One of the most beautiful nuances of this icon is the hands of Jesus grabbing the wrists of Adam and Eve. When you shake hands with someone, it denotes a sense of equality. But grabbing someone by the wrist denotes that the person grabbing is doing most of the work in uniting the two people. You can carry someone by the wrist in a firmer way than you can by the hand. As I see this icon and the grabbing of the wrists, I like to think this means that Jesus is willing to meet us more than halfway. Adam and Eve had to offer their hands—they had to do something—but their reaching as an act of faith is rewarded by Christ in grabbing them and pulling them to Himself.

We can't meet Christ halfway. We are not His equal. However, He does not impose Himself on our lives. He sacrificed His life willingly for us, and He wants us to make it to the Kingdom of heaven. He is rooting for us. Salvation is ours to lose. But we must have some amount of faith and some amount of work to prepare to meet the Lord. We have to reach out in faith. We have to back up that faith with work. We need to believe in the goodness of God and humbly ask for His grace. We need to repent of what we've done wrong and use the time we have left to do better, to serve, to be a good steward of the time we've been given.

Christ Is Risen, and There Is Hope

If people know only one hymn of the church, it is this one: "Christ is Risen from the dead, by death trampling down upon death, and to those in the tombs He has granted life." This hymn is only twenty-two words long, and four of those words carry a negative connotation—*dead, death, death, tombs*. Yet this is the most joyful hymn of the church year. At the Resurrection service each Pascha we sing it dozens of times, so that it seeps into the consciousness of each person, a hymn stuck in everyone's head. We sing it for forty days, many times at each service, to emphasize its meaning. This hymn neither praises God (doxology) nor asks Him for anything (supplication). Rather, it is a teaching hymn—it reminds us why the journey was important after the long struggle of Great Lent and Holy Week.

It summarizes for us the meaning of life. If Christ is not risen from the Tomb, indeed life is a slow march to nothing. But because Christ is risen, there is hope for you and for me: There is an objective, there is a destination, there is a goal. And our life purpose then becomes accepting the message and preparing for the destination.

When I visit someone for what I know will be the last time, when I say my good-byes to them and offer a prayer for a Christian, painless, blameless, and peaceful end to their lives, the last thing I do, no matter what day of the year it is, is sing the hymn "Christ is Risen." I want the last thing that someone hears from me, the Church, and the God I serve to be "and to those in the tombs He has granted life." For the one about to pass from life, there should be conviction (probably mixed with some trepidation) that death is not an end of everything, but a transition to something greater.

The day I was ordained, and on many days still to this day, I felt— and feel—overwhelmed doing what I do: placing my hands on the Holy Gifts of God, unworthy as I am. Yet, I am comforted by the thought that someone has to step forward and be a priest. Otherwise there would be no priests and no Church. It's the same with the prospect of eternal life. No one is worthy to claim heaven. It is the gift of God to each who receives it. Yet we have the sacrifice of Christ and the promise of God to help us know that the Kingdom of heaven is possible. And so we continue on, hopefully as a good steward of each day with which God blesses us.

I hope that you've gotten something out of this book. I hope you know more and fear less. I hope you are more convicted in your faith and resolved to be a better steward. I hope the stories of pious people presented in this book give you hope and inspiration. If you've made a mess of life, I hope the story of the repentant thief will reassure you that it's never too late, while we are still alive on earth, to get this right. If your life resembles the poor man Lazarus, I hope you will be reassured that your patience will be rewarded.

Most of all, I hope this book has given you pause to think and to reflect on the most important event of our lives: our passing from this life into eternal life. The goal of a painless, blameless, and peaceful end, prepared for a good accounting before the awesome judgment seat of Christ, is on the table for all of us—spoken about at each Divine Liturgy, hopefully in our thoughts frequently, and then prepared for with everlasting hope in the everlasting goodness and mercy of the Good Lord.

The Church is wise and kind. It speaks of the goal and destination constantly in the services so that as the years go by and the birthdays accumulate, we aren't left with sadness as we watch the sand empty from the hourglass of our lives on earth. Instead, we have faith that the door each of us will pass through at the end of our life can, by faith, work, and grace, open the door to a greater life than we could ever imagine. Jesus is extending His hand. You just need to raise yours. That requires faith, and it requires work, and it requires His grace, which He so willingly extends.

Jesus is extending His hand. He is eager for you and me to raise ours.

I will extol Thee, O Lord, for thou has drawn me up,
    and hast not let my foes rejoice over me.
O Lord my God, I cried to thee for help,
    and thou hast healed me.
O Lord, thou hast brought up my soul from Sheol,
    restored me to life among those gone down to the Pit.

Sing praises to the Lord, O you his saints,
    and give thanks to his holy name.
Sing praises to the Lord, O you His saints,
    and give thanks to His holy name.
For his anger is but for a moment,
    and his favor is for a lifetime.

Weeping may tarry for the night,
   but joy comes with the morning.

As for me, I said in my prosperity,
   "I shall never be moved."
By thy favor, O LORD,
   thou hadst established me as a strong mountain;
thou didst hide thy face,
   I was dismayed.

To thee, O LORD, I cried;
   and to the LORD I made supplication:
"What profit is there in my death,
   if I go down to the Pit?
Will the dust praise thee?
   Will it tell of thy faithfulness?
Hear, O LORD, and be gracious to me!
   O LORD, be thou my helper!"

Thou hast turned for me my mourning into dancing;
   thou hast loosed my sackcloth
   and girded me with gladness,
that my soul may praise Thee and not be silent.
   O LORD, my God, I will give thanks to thee for ever.
(*Psalm 30*)

Christ is Risen! Truly He is Risen!

   To Him be the glory, the dominion, and the power to the
ages of ages. Amen.

Memorial Prayer from the
Orthodox Funeral Service[49]

O God of spirits and of all flesh, You trampled upon death and abolished the power of the devil, giving life to Your world. Give rest to the soul(s) of Your departed servant(s) (their names) in a place of light, in a place of green pasture, in a place of refreshment, from where pain, sorrow and sighing have fled away. As a good and loving God, forgive every sin he (she, they) has (have) committed in word, deed or thought, for there is no one who lives and does not sin. You alone are without sin. Your righteousness is an everlasting righteousness, and Your word is truth. For You are the resurrection, the life, and the repose of Your departed servant(s) (their names), Christ our God, and to You we offer up glory, with Your eternal Father who is without beginning and Your all-holy, good, and life-creating Spirit, now and forever and to the ages of ages. Amen.

---

49 *The Divine Liturgy of St. John Chrysostom* (2015), 117.

The Paschal Homily of
St. John Chrysostom[50]

Whosoever is a devout lover of God, let him enjoy this beautiful bright Festival. And whosoever is a grateful servant, let him joyously enter into the joy of his Lord. And if any be weary with fasting, let him now receive his reward. If any has toiled from the first hour let him receive his just debt. If any came after the third let him gratefully celebrate. If any arrived after the sixth, let him not doubt; for he too shall sustain no loss. If any have delayed to the ninth, let him come without hesitation. If any arrived only at the eleventh hour, let him not be afraid by reason of his delay; for the Master is gracious and receives the last, even as the first. He gives rest to him who arrives at the eleventh hour, as well as him who has labored from the first. He is merciful to the one who delays and nourishes the first. He gives also to the one, and to the other He is gracious. He accepts the works, as He greets the endeavor, He honors the deed, and the intent He commends.

Let all of you then enter into the joy of your Lord. The first and second enjoy your reward. You rich and poor, rejoice together. You temperate and you heedless, honor the day. You who fasted, and you who did not, rejoice today. The table is richly laden. All of you, fare

---

50 *Holy Week—Pascha*, trans. Fr. George Papadeas (Patmos Press, 2011), 481–82.

sumptuously on it. The Calf is a fatted one; let no one go away hungry. All of you enjoy the banquet of faith. All of you enjoy the riches of His goodness. Let no one grieve poverty; for the universal Kingdom has been revealed.

Let no one grieve over sins; for forgiveness has dawned from the tomb. Let no one fear death; for the Death of our Savior has set us free. He has destroyed it by enduring it. He despoiled Hades, when He descended thereto. He embittered it, having tasted of His flesh. Isaiah foretold this when he cried out: "You, O Hades, have been embittered by encountering Him below." It was embittered, for it was abolished. It was embittered, for it was mocked. It was embittered, for it was slain. It was embittered, for it was annihilated. It was embittered, for it is now made captive. It took a body, and, lo, it discovered God. It took earth and, behold! It encountered Heaven. It took what it saw, and was overcome by what it could not see. O death, where is your sting? O Hades, where is your victory? Christ is risen, and you are annihilated. Christ is risen, and the demons have fallen. Christ is risen, and the Angels rejoice. Christ is risen, and life is liberated. Christ is risen, and the tomb is emptied of the dead; for Christ, having risen from the dead, has become the first fruits of those who fall asleep. To Him be the glory and the dominion to the Ages of Ages. Amen.

Acknowledgments

In February 2015, a member of my parish approached me with an idea about creating a prayer team of parishioners who would commit to praying for the church and for me on a daily basis during the upcoming Lenten period. I have always enjoyed writing, and I decided that I would write a daily reflection and send it to whomever joined the prayer team. I had hoped that thirty people would participate, and my intention was to do this for forty days. Over 150 people joined the prayer team, and as Lent came to an end, they asked me if I would continue the daily reflections. So I did.

Now, many years into this practice, I write on various topics related to prayer, the Orthodox Faith, and the Christian life. This is the tenth book that has come out of the daily reflections for the prayer team.

I wish to thank those who have helped and encouraged me in this project:

His Eminence Metropolitan Sevastianos of Atlanta, of the Greek Orthodox Archdiocese of America, for his prayers and blessings.

Ancient Faith Publishing for offering me a chance to publish this book under their name: to Melinda Johnson for signing off on this project; to Donna Ryan for coordinating this project; to Lynnette Horner and Deacon Irenaios Anderson for their invaluable help in painstakingly editing the manuscript.

The many parishioners of St. John the Baptist Greek Orthodox Church in Tampa, Florida, for their support of the prayer team and encouragement to move forward with this project.

All the members of the prayer team for reading my reflections, for your prayers, and for your encouragement.

The Orthodox Christian Network (OCN) for posting my writings.

My parents, Nicholas and Barbara (of blessed memory), for taking me to church faithfully, for encouraging me to serve in the altar, and for helping me to develop my writing skills.

My son, Nicholas, who already enjoys writing, for his unconditional love and for the beautiful stories he tells.

My wife, Lisa, for her support of my ministry, for the many sacrifices she makes for our family, and for her encouragement to write.

The many families that have invited me into the most intimate seasons of their lives, allowing me to be present in the final moments of their loved ones and trusting me to guide them to have a meaningful parting.

Finally, and most especially, I thank the Lord for the great blessing to serve as a Greek Orthodox priest, for the privilege of ministering to people in the final days and moments of their lives, and for allowing me to see miracles even in death. I thank Him for providing me the thoughts and the words that I pray have brought comfort in these most difficult moments.

Because he cleaves to me in love, I will deliver him;
I will protect him, because he knows my name.
When he calls to me, I will answer him;
I will be with him in trouble,
I will rescue him and honor him.
With long life I will satisfy him,
and show Him my salvation.
Psalm 91:14–16

Books by Fr. Stavros Akrotirianakis

Blessed Is the Kingdom: Reflections on the Divine Liturgy of St. John Chrysostom (Ancient Faith Publishing, 2024)

The Greatest Story Ever Sung: Reflections on the Hymns of Holy Week in the Orthodox Church (Xulon Press, 2023)

The Heart of Encouragement: 176 Reflections to Build You Up and Empower You to Build Up Others (Xulon Press, 2022)

Commissioned to Be Apostles: Love, Worship, Community, Learning, Service (Xulon Press, 2022)

Unto the Healing of Soul and Body: Encouragement for Restoration and Reconciliation in a Broken World (Holy Cross Orthodox Press, 2022)

Engaged: The Call to Be Disciples: Reflections on What It Means to Be a Christian (Xulon Press, 2021)

Let Us Be Attentive: Reflections on the Sunday and Feast Day Scripture Readings of the Orthodox Church (Xulon Press, 2019)

Let All Creation Rejoice: Reflections on Advent, the Nativity and Epiphany (Xulon Press, 2016)

The Road Back to Christ: Reflections on Lent, Holy Week and the Resurrection (Xulon Press, 2016)

We hope you have enjoyed and benefited from this book. Your financial support makes it possible to continue our nonprofit ministry both in print and online. Because the proceeds from our book sales only partially cover the costs of operating **Ancient Faith Publishing** and **Ancient Faith Radio**, we greatly appreciate the generosity of our readers and listeners. Donations are tax deductible and can be made at **www.ancientfaith.com.**

To view our other publications,
please visit our website: **store.ancientfaith.com**

Bringing you Orthodox Christian music, readings, prayers,
teaching, and podcasts 24 hours a day since 2004 at
www.ancientfaith.com